Grafted In

ISRAEL, GENTILES,
AND THE MYSTERY OF THE GOSPEL

Grafted In

ISRAEL, GENTILES,
AND THE MYSTERY OF THE GOSPEL

D. Thomas Lancaster

Second Edition, formerly titled *The Mystery of the Gospel*
Revised with a new introduction and two new chapters.

FIRST FRUITS OF
ZION

Second Edition 2009
Printed in the United States of America

First Edition 2003, First Fruits of Zion, published under the title
The Mystery of the Gospel: Jew and Gentile and the Eternal Purpose of God

ISBN Softcover: 978–1–892124–35–7
ISBN Hardcover: 978–1–892124–36–4

Unless otherwise noted, Scripture quotations are from the New
International Version®, © Copyright 1973, 1978, 1984 by International
Bible Society. Throughout this publication the name Jesus is rendered
Yeshua and Christ is rendered Messiah.

Cover Design: Avner Wolff

Quantity discounts are available on bulk purchases of this book for
educational, fundraising, or event purposes. Special versions or book
excerpts to fit specific needs are available from First Fruits of Zion. For more
information, contact www.ffoz.org/contact.

First Fruits of Zion

PO Box 649, Marshfield, Missouri 65706–0649 USA
Phone (417) 468–2741, www.ffoz.org

Comments and questions: www.ffoz.org/contact

TO MY NOBLE WIFE

אשת חיל

AND SOUL COMPANION

CONTENTS

INTRODUCTION
THE SECOND EDITION

Gentile Believers Have a Place in Israel—Or Do They?

G entile believers have a place in Israel. That was the audacious premise of this book when First Fruits of Zion released it under the title *The Mystery of the Gospel: Jews, Gentiles, and the Eternal Purpose of God.* In retrospect, I think that simple message blurred an important line of distinction between Jews and Gentiles, a line that the apostles maintained. In this brief introduction to the second edition of the book, I hope to clarify what I mean when I say that Gentiles have a place in Israel.

This is a book for Messianic Gentiles. This book was originally intended to address a rift in the Messianic Jewish movement. In the year 2001, I saw a local Messianic Jewish congregation split and divide over a new teaching called "Two-House Theology." I sifted through a pile of literature—books, articles, arguments—generated by those advancing the new theology and by those opposing it. In summary, the brand of Two-House Theology that I encountered taught that most Gentile believers in North America were descendants of the ten lost tribes of Israel because of the genetic dispersion of those tribes through the centuries. The conclusion was that Gentile believers have as much right to call themselves "Israel" as Jews do.

At the time, I was a freelance writer for First Fruits of Zion. I made a telephone call to Boaz Michael and asked him if we should be addressing the matter. He suggested that I write a book about it. Rather than challenge the lost-tribes theory directly, I wanted to demonstrate to our readers that a Gentile believer has status in Israel through Messiah. Paul's gospel of Gentile inclusion caused a ruckus in the apostolic age. I felt that it would be healthier for Gentile believers in the Messianic movement to find their sense of identity in Messiah rather than a presumed genetic connection to the lost tribes. The result was *The Mystery of the Gospel*, an examination of Paul's theology regarding Gentile participation in Israel. The book was not an academic work, nor was it a systematic argument. Though the issues under discussion were sometimes nuanced and specialized, I tried to write a book that could be read and enjoyed by the average reader.

Five years after its release, we have decided to reprint the book. The reprint has given me the opportunity to make changes. As I reviewed the original manuscript, I became concerned that my oft-repeated message, "Gentile believers have a place in Israel," could easily be misconstrued as something I did not intend.

Israel-According-to-the-Flesh

"Israel" might refer to several different things. It is the name God gave Jacob and another name for the biblical patriarch Jacob. It can refer to the descendants of Jacob, the "sons of Israel" whom Moses led through the wilderness and to the promised land. It can refer to that promised land—the land of Israel. It can refer to the united kingdom of tribes under the administration of King Saul, King David, and King Solomon, or it might refer to just the ten northern tribes that broke off from the monarchy of David. It might refer to the Jewish people who returned from exile, or it might refer to everyone who practices the Jewish religion: Judaism.

To which of these Israels am I referring when I claim that Gentile believers have a place in Israel?

The difficulty arises because I failed to make a clear distinction between what I should have termed "Legal Israel" and "Kingdom Israel." Paul makes the distinction explicit. For example, when writing to the Corinthians—a community composed of both Jewish and Gentile believers—he says, "Consider Israel-according-to-the-flesh. Are not those who eat from the sacrifices part of the fellowship of the altar?" (1 Corinthians 10:18, my translation).

In this verse, Paul refers to Israel as a group distinct from the Corinthian assembly. He speaks as if the Corinthians are on the outside of this group. He also adds a qualifier to the term Israel: he calls it "Israel-according-to-the-flesh."

In 1 Corinthians 10:18, Israel-according-to-the-flesh is composed of those individuals who may eat of the holy sacrifices. In Paul's day, that group consisted only of those who were halachically (legally) Jewish. Paul was defining Israel-according-to-the-flesh as those who were born Jewish or who had undergone a legal conversion into Judaism: "both Jews and converts to Judaism."[1]

Why did Paul feel it necessary to add the qualifier "according to the flesh" when describing those who were legally Jewish? Why not just say "Israel"?

The qualifier must have been necessary because the Corinthians also had an identity in the generic term Israel. If there is an "Israel-according-to-the-flesh," there must be an "Israel-not-according-to-the-flesh." The not-according-to-the-flesh version would have been the believers, including the Corinthians.

At the beginning of 1 Corinthians 10, Paul referred to the generation of Israelites who followed Moses as the "forefathers" of the Corinthian believers. To Paul, the Corinthians were part of Israel. Yet the Gentile Corinthians could not access the Temple or participate in the sacrificial services. Therefore, he found it necessary to make a distinction between those who were legally identified as Israel and his broader use of the term. If that had not been the case, he need not have made the clarification "Israel-according-to-the-flesh."

The implication of Paul's use of the language is that if natural-born Jews and circumcised proselytes are "Israel-according-to-the-flesh," then the Gentiles in Messiah must belong to a broader definition of Israel. Paul usually places "spirit" in antithesis to "flesh," so we could call it "spiritual Israel," but I prefer the term "Kingdom Israel." For purposes of this introduction, "Kingdom Israel" should be understood to signify both legal Israel and the Gentile believers.

Paul did not use the terms "spiritual Israel" or "Kingdom Israel." Instead, he introduced two new terms to describe the Kingdom

Israel that includes the Gentiles of faith: "Israel of God" and "Commonwealth of Israel."

ISRAEL OF GOD

In Galatians, Paul used the term "Israel of God" to encompass legal Israel and those who had become Abraham's children through faith:

> Neither circumcision nor uncircumcision means anything; what counts is a new creation. Peace and mercy to all who follow this rule, even to the Israel of God. (Galatians 6:15–16)

The use of the term "Israel of God" in Galatians is remarkable because it comes at the conclusion of a long treatise on why it is unnecessary for Gentile believers to become circumcised proselytes. Through the argument in Galatians, Paul maintains that Gentiles have become "sons of Abraham" (a technical term for proselytes) through faith. Paul uses the term "Israel of God" to imply something more than simply legal Israel in the conventional sense. It may also imply that Paul would not have been comfortable telling the Galatian Gentiles, "You have a place in Israel," without further qualification. Instead, he would say, "You have a place in the Israel of God."

COMMONWEALTH OF ISRAEL

In Ephesians 2:12 Paul uses the term "Commonwealth of Israel" while discussing the Gentile inclusion and the status of Gentile believers as fellow citizens with Jews. If Paul felt that faith in Yeshua gave the Gentiles legal status in natural Israel, this would have been the place to say so. He did not. Instead he used broader terminology:

> Ye were at that time apart from [the Messiah], having been alienated from the commonwealth of Israel. (Ephesians 2:12 YLT)

> Then, therefore, ye are no more strangers and foreigners, but fellow-citizens of the saints, and of the household of God. (Ephesians 2:19 YLT)

In these two verses, the term "commonwealth of Israel" is placed parallel to the terms "saints" and "the household of God."

The Greek word translated as "commonwealth" is rendered as "citizenship" in the NIV. The concepts of "commonwealth" and "citizenship" were familiar to Paul. The Apostle Paul was a Jew from Tarsus, yet he had Roman citizenship. Though he had full participation in Rome and fell under the jurisdiction of Roman law, he retained his ethnic identity as a Jew. He did not live in Rome, but both Tarsus and Jerusalem were cities within the Roman Empire. He seems to have looked at a Gentile believer's relationship to Israel in similar terms.

Paul and the apostles were looking forward to a future day when the powerful Roman Empire would be replaced by the kingdom of Messiah. The apostles believed that in the coming kingdom, Messiah will reign over the entire earth as the King of Israel. The kingdom of Israel will be the imperial power over all Gentiles. Paul viewed Gentile believers in Messiah as citizens of that future kingdom of Israel. Though they were not Jewish, they attained citizenship in Kingdom Israel, just as non-Roman subjects of the Roman Empire (like himself) could attain Roman citizenship.

IN THE EYES OF MEN

I hope that these citations are sufficient to demonstrate that in Paul's mind, there was a real distinction between legal Israel and Kingdom Israel. In Paul's theology (and that of the apostles) the distinction between legal Israel and Kingdom Israel has some practical ramifications in the realm of Gentile obligation to observe Torah. If there were not a discernable difference between Jewish and Gentile legal status, the legislation in Acts 15 would have been unnecessary.

In Acts 15 and 21, the apostles affirmed that obedience to Torah is absolutely mandatory and binding for Jewish believers. But they granted Gentile believers significant space. The Gentile believers were placed on the trajectory of Torah by Acts 15, the writings of Paul, and discipleship to Yeshua, but Paul and the other apostles were unwilling to place the Gentiles under the full obligation of conversion into legal Israel because that was wrongly understood as a prerequisite for salvation.

Paul implies a difference between legal Israel and Kingdom Israel in Romans 2 when he distinguishes between one who is only Jewish "outwardly," according to the flesh, and one who is Jewish inwardly:

> For he is not a Jew who is so outwardly, neither is circumcision that which is outward in flesh; but a Jew is he who is so inwardly, and circumcision is of the heart, in spirit, not in letter, of which the praise is not of men, but of God. (Romans 2:28–29 YLT)

Paul concedes that a Gentile who is a Jew "inwardly" and therefore part of Kingdom Israel (but not legal Israel) has no legal standing in Israel in the eyes of men. Therefore, his "praise is not of men, but of God."

The main borderline between natural Israel and Kingdom Israel, according to Paul, is not Torah observance. Instead, it is a status he refers to as "in the eyes of men." He frequently refers to those who are a part of legal Israel as having approval "in the eyes of men." In the world of Judaism today, we would refer to this as "halachic status." Paul does not seem to regard legal, halachic status as carrying a great deal of weight before God. He says, "Circumcision is nothing and uncircumcision is nothing. Keeping God's commands is what counts" (1 Corinthians 7:19).

MESSIANIC GENTILES

Back to the original question: What does this book mean when it says, "Gentile believers have a place in Israel"? It means that, in the eyes of God, Gentile believers have been adopted into his people. It does not mean that Gentiles have legal standing as Jews, nor does it mean that Christians are the new Israel. Instead, Gentile believers are part of a greater collective that is variously called the Israel of God, the Commonwealth of Israel, the Assembly, the people of God, and the kingdom of heaven. The olive tree into which the Gentile believers of Romans 11 are engrafted is the nation of Israel.

This position in Israel does not make a Gentile believer Jewish, but it makes him a fellow citizen in Kingdom Israel along with his Jewish brothers and sisters. As a member of the household of Israel, the Gentile believer should not be deterred from the practice of Messianic Judaism. Participation in Torah is the natural mode of faith expression for a member of Israel, whether a person be a member of Israel-according-to-the-flesh or Kingdom Israel.

I have made small editorial changes for the second edition throughout the book, but the main content and conclusions remain the same. We have changed the title from *The Mystery of the Gospel: Jews, Gentiles, and the Eternal Purpose of God* to the somewhat less abstract *Grafted In: Israel, Gentiles, and the Mystery of the Gospel.*

Also included in this edition are two lectures I presented at the 2008 First Fruits of Zion national conference in Hudson, WI. The lectures, titled "We Were in a Synagogue" and "To Pray as a Gentile," are tangentially related to the theme of Gentile participation in Messianic Judaism and seemed appropriate for publication in this volume.

As the book goes into its second printing, I hope that it can continue to be an encouragement for those brave souls who have chosen to walk the lonely path of the Messianic Gentile. I hope it will encourage Two-House readers to root their identity first and foremost in Yeshua. I hope it will encourage Messianic Jews to take pride in their heritage and to open their doors to their brothers and sisters from the nations who are being drawn toward their light.

INTRODUCTION
THE FIRST EDITION
(REVISED)

The Pilgrimage

Blessed are those whose strength is in you,
Who have set their hearts on pilgrimage.
They go from strength to strength,
Till each appears before God in Zion. (Psalm 84:5, 7)

To what can the kingdom be compared? It can be compared to a pilgrimage up to Jerusalem.

Such pilgrimages happened three times a year. For the holy festivals of Passover, Pentecost, and Tabernacles, all Israel went up to the Temple. The Mishnah[2] describes the caravans of pilgrims who gathered in the villages and cities of Israel in preparation for the journey to Jerusalem. Friends and family, neighbors and countrymen, met in the villages of assembly. Final provisions for the journey were purchased. Bags were packed. Prayers for safety were prayed. Overnight the pilgrims transformed the village into a city of tents. Some slept under the wheeling stars of the open sky.

At dawn the head of the assembly awoke the pilgrims by shouting into the early morning air, "Arise, let us go up to Zion, to the House of the LORD our God!" (Jeremiah 31:6). The glad song began.

A flute player led the way. They sang their way to Jerusalem. The miles were many and long, under the sun by day, under the moon by night. Always climbing to higher ground, up into the hill country of Judah. The travelers met other caravans of pilgrims. They joined their voices together and continued the song-filled journey. Their feet were weary, but their hearts were light. The closer they came to the holy city, the more crowded the roads became. "Multitudes of people from a multitude of cities flowed in an endless stream to the holy Temple … from the east and west, from the north and south."[3]

As the roads filled with people, distinctions of village, clan, and tribe were blurred and quickly forgotten. When at last they laid eyes upon Jerusalem—resplendent, white stone bathed in sunlight—a cheer rose from the travelers. Before them was the Temple of the LORD.

A pilgrimage to a festival in Jerusalem is a particularly apt metaphor for the people of God. In a pilgrimage, everyone on the road began at a different point of origin and now occupies a different place on the journey, but will one day be joined in one place of glad worship. So too, the people of God, comprised of members from many different beginnings, now occupy many different positions on the journey, but ultimately arrive at the same goal. The journey itself is not the goal, but the journey is the means to the goal. Anyone can join the journey, and our joy will not be complete until everyone on the journey has arrived at the destination.

This is a book about people on the journey of Messianic Judaism. It is not a book about how to join the journey or why the journey should be made. Those would be topics for other books. Rather, this book deals with the realization that we are not alone on this journey. There are other people on the road. There are other people practicing Messianic Judaism. Some of them do not look like us. Some of them do. Some of them seem to be family members; others seem to be strangers from far away. Somehow, we have all been swept up together into something bigger than ourselves. Our individual journeys have been merged into one great movement of people.

That's what this book is about. Some are wondering if perhaps it would be better for all parties involved if this mass of people were separated into distinct caravans. We could divide it along ethnic lines, or we might divide it along historical religious lines. "Jews should be Jews; Gentiles should be Gentiles." Some have become so enamored of the Jewish pilgrims that they have spurned their own clans and forgotten their own families. "I must be Jewish too," they say. Others have fallen under the impression that differences between the travelers on the road are only superficial and that we are all long-lost relatives. Many on the journey have demanded that the old family ways be set aside. "Enough with all this glad singing. You Jews must accept the fact that you are Christians now, and we sing a different melody," they say. "After all, this journey is no longer your journey; it is ours."

Recent years have seen significant progress in establishing a biblical basis for Jewish identity in Messiah. Biblical scholarship has begun to jettison the old theologies that taught that Jews have no place in the kingdom of heaven short of abandoning Torah and converting to Christianity. The Jewish believer in Messiah is now recognized as the normal expectation of the Apostolic Scriptures, not the exception to the rule.

Messianic Judaism has birthed a theology of "Torah Christianity," a return to the prototype of apostolic-era, biblical faith and observance. This return, however, has stopped short of affirming the full participation of both Jews and non-Jews. The prevailing conventional wisdom remains that Jewish believers should do Jewish things (like Torah and Shabbat), while Gentile believers should do Gentile things (like attending church on Sunday and participating in traditional Christian forms of worship).

Those non-Jews who have taken up the call to shoulder the Master's yoke have found themselves trapped in a no-man's-land—stuck somewhere between Messianic Judaism (which often refuses participation for other ethnicities) and the mainstream churches (which do not acknowledge the relevance of Torah in a believer's life). The message from both parties is that Jews should be Jews and Christians should be Christians.

It is not my intention to suggest that Gentile believers are "Jewish." I understand the term "Jew" or "Jewish" to mean people who trace their family connections to the ancient people of Israel, whether through ancestry or through legal conversion into normative Judaism. Neither is it my intention to suggest that Gentile believers should co-opt Jewish culture and tradition. I am a firm believer in the diversity of the body, and it pains me to see Jewish identity eroded by believers who carelessly bandy about Judaica as if those external things were the fullest expression of Torah life. Yet at the same time, for Messianic Judaism to deny Gentile disciples of Yeshua participation among the greater commonwealth of Israel is wrong.

As a lifelong Gentile myself and as a teacher in a Messianic Jewish congregation with a Gentile majority in attendance, I have been over this ground a few times. This book specifically addresses the position of the Gentile believer within the people of Israel, within Messianic Judaism, and within the kingdom of heaven.

Perhaps the primary question that vexes Gentile believers in a Messianic Jewish context is not so much one of theological identity as much as a question of "How do I fit into the story?" After all, our Scriptures come to us as a more-or-less continuous, historical narrative detailing the lives and adventures of God's chosen people. The book of Genesis is built on collections of stories called the *toledot* (genealogies) of the people of God. The genealogies include family trees that contain the details of who begat whom while also telling the histories of how God interacted with both "who" and "whom." For the Jewish believer, these genealogies are deeply personal because they are the stories of his family, and if he diligently peers into them, he can discern his own place in the sprawling family tree of Jewish and biblical history.

For the Gentile believer the relationship is not immediately obvious. We wonder if Abraham is really *our* father. If so, are Isaac and Jacob also? Is the LORD really "the God of *my* fathers" or is he "the God of *their* fathers"? We wonder if we have permission to partake in the Torah. Does our salvation, in one sense or another, make us Jewish? Am I an Israelite?

I hope to answer some of these questions of identity that may haunt Gentile followers of the Jewish Messiah. I expect that Jewish readers will enjoy the book as well, and perhaps even find their own place in the stories in ways they had not previously considered. This book, then, is meant for everyone practicing Messianic Judaism. It is for everyone on the road to Zion, for everyone on the journey. It is meant for all of us—the First Fruits of Zion.

NEXT YEAR IN JERUSALEM,
D. THOMAS LANCASTER

1
THE MYSTERY OF THE GOSPEL

Ephesians

He is an old and worn Jew chained to an armed guard. For two years, he has been under house arrest while waiting for his trial before Nero. If nothing else, the incarceration has given him some time to think. He has had time to mull over the events of his ministry. He has had time to weigh the significance of his amazing journeys and the amazing message of the gospel he has been proclaiming. He has had time to think about why he is wearing chains.

Many of Paul's musings find their best expression in his prison epistles written to the Ephesians and to the Colossians. In those two letters, the apostle gives us a sense of his own perspective on the gospel and the consequences of his ministry to the nations. He sums up his life's calling and attempts to illuminate what he considers to be the deepest mystery of the gospel.

In Ephesians chapter 6 Paul writes, "Pray also for me, that whenever I open my mouth, words may be given me so that I will fearlessly make known the mystery of the gospel, for which I am an ambassador in chains."[4] What then is the "mystery of the gospel"? Why, exactly, was Paul in chains?

ARREST IN JERUSALEM

One would naturally assume that the "mystery of the gospel" for which Paul was in chains is the message of Messiah's death and resurrection. After all, that is the good news that Paul proclaimed. One could assume this, but one would be wrong.

Paul had been part of the pilgrimage to the festival of Pentecost (Shavuot) in Jerusalem. While in the Temple preparing for the festival, he was arrested. His arrest did not come as the result of his preaching the death and resurrection of Yeshua. At the time of Paul's arrest, James the brother of the Master was also in Jerusalem preaching the same gospel, as were thousands of believing Jews, all of them "zealous for the Torah."[5] None of them was being arrested, dragged before the Sanhedrin, marched off to Caesarea, or sent to Rome. Paul was arrested for spreading a message even more controversial than the resurrection of Yeshua.

The mob of pilgrims assaulting Paul in the Temple was not incited because he was preaching the gospel. At the time of Paul's arrest, the believers were a tolerated, albeit frowned-upon, sect of Jerusalem Judaism. So why was Paul attacked by an angry mob in the Temple? The charge leveled against him was that he had brought Gentiles into the Temple. The Acts narrative records the charge against him: "He has brought Greeks into the Temple area and defiled this Holy Place."[6] Luke immediately clarifies for us that the charge was untrue: "They had previously seen Trophimus the Ephesian in the city with Paul and assumed that Paul had brought him into the Temple area."[7]

Not that Gentiles weren't allowed into the Temple's outer courts. The largest of all the Temple's courts was the great court of the Gentiles. Men and women from all nations routinely ascended to the top of the Temple Mount and congregated in the court of the Gentiles. There they could worship the God of Israel in his Holy House, a house of prayer for all nations. They could not, however, proceed from the court of the Gentiles and enter into the Temple proper. A dividing wall stood between the Gentile worshipper and the inner courts of the Temple. Jews were allowed to go in as far as the altar of burnt offering. Gentiles could only look on from a distance.

Josephus writes about the dividing wall of partition, "There was a partition made of stone all around, whose height was three cubits; its construction was very elegant; upon it stood pillars, at equal distances from one another, declaring the law of purity, some in Greek, and some in Roman letters, that 'no foreigner should go within that sanctuary.'"[8] In another place, he says it was "a stone wall for a partition, with an inscription, which forbade any foreigner to go in under pain of death."[9]

In Acts 21, Paul was bringing sacrifices for purification and for the completion of a vow. In order to do so, he had to enter the Temple up to the very court of Israel. As he was passing from the court of the Gentiles and into the courts of Israel, he was seen by several Jews from Asia Minor. They had earlier seen Paul around Jerusalem with Trophimus the Ephesian—a Gentile.

The Jews from Asia Minor knew Paul. They knew that he was flooding the synagogues all over Asia Minor with Gentiles, because those were their own synagogues. They knew something of his theology regarding Gentiles, if not the details of it. They at least knew enough to be certain that they did not like him. Naturally, they assumed that Paul was bringing Gentiles with him into the Temple area even as he had brought so many Gentiles into their own synagogues. They assumed that Paul was now here in Jerusalem bringing his beloved Gentiles past the dividing wall and into the very court of Israel.

The ensuing riot was serious enough to elicit a response from Jerusalem's Roman garrison. If not for a quick rescue by soldiers from Fortress Antonia, Paul might not have survived. The commander of the garrison sent troops into the middle of the crowd to pluck Paul out from the fray. They bound him with two chains and tried to ascertain from the crowd exactly what it was that Paul had done and why everyone wanted to beat the stuffing out of him. The crowd was so heated up that the soldiers had to lift Paul onto their shoulders and carry him back to the fortress. What a scene—bound with two heavy chains and carried out of the Temple courts like a sack of potatoes.

When they reached the steps of the fortress, Paul received permission to turn and address the crowd. Hands still bound with heavy chains, he motioned for silence. At last, when his would-be lynchers were quiet, he told his story.

He told them he was a Jew, a Pharisee discipled under Gamaliel. *The* Gamaliel.[10] He told them his testimony: how he was a persecutor of the believing Jews, how he was on his way to Damascus, how he was blinded and encountered Messiah as a voice from heaven, how he had to be led by the hand to Damascus.

The crowd made no objections to any of these comments. There were no shouts of "Blasphemy!" or jeers at the mention of a voice from heaven belonging to Yeshua. Even the issue of Yeshua's messianic office was met with respectful attention. None of those seemingly controversial claims proved to be the hot button that would raise the mob's ire.

Paul continued his story. He told about how his vision was restored through Ananias's prayer. He told about his immersion into Yeshua and his return to Jerusalem. He told about praying in the Temple and seeing a vision of Yeshua speaking with him in the Temple. To all of this the crowd still had no objection—not until Paul recounted Yeshua saying to him, "Go; I will send you far away to the Gentiles," did the crowd object. The Gentile thing was the hot button.

No sooner did Paul mention that he was sent to the Gentiles than we read, "The crowd listened to Paul until he said this. Then they raised their voices and shouted, 'Rid the earth of him! He's not fit to live!'" Paul's mission to the Gentiles was the issue that triggered the riot. It was not the gospel of the death, resurrection, and messianic office of Yeshua for which Paul was nearly beaten to death and arrested. Rather, it was the message of the inclusion of Gentiles that brought the wrath of Jerusalem onto his head.

The Gentile inclusion in Israel, through the Messiah of Israel, was the real offense of the gospel to Jewish ears. Paul understood this well. In Galatians 5:11 he made that plain by pointing out that if circumcision was a prerequisite to salvation, then "the offense of the cross has been abolished." What is the offense of the cross? From Paul's perspective in Galatians, the offense of the cross is Gentile inclusion in Israel.

It was for the offense of the gospel (that is, the offensive idea of Gentile inclusion) that Paul had been arrested, tried before the Sanhedrin, marched to Caesarea, and subsequently shipped to Rome. When Paul writes in Ephesians that he is an ambassador in chains for the mystery of the gospel, we are given an important clue to that mystery. Paul was not in chains for preaching Messiah; he was in chains for preaching Gentile inclusion through Messiah. The mystery of the gospel, for which Paul was in chains, was the Gentile inclusion.[11]

Brothers, Sons of Abraham, and God-fearing Gentiles

Paul's mission to the Gentiles began to raise trouble for him even before he referred to himself as the apostle to the nations. As early as Acts 13, we learn that Paul's inclusive attitude toward Gentiles is going to cause problems. Acts 13 tells the story of Paul and Barnabas attending a synagogue service in the province of Galatia, in the city of Pisidian Antioch. After the reading from the Torah and the Prophets, the synagogue officials invited Paul, the visiting rabbi from Jerusalem, to present a teaching. Paul stood up and delivered a stirring defense of the messianic faith in Yeshua. The congregation received the sermon well. The book of Acts tells us, "The people invited them to speak further about these things on the next Sabbath. When the congregation was dismissed, many of the Jews and devout converts to Judaism followed Paul and Barnabas, who talked with them and urged them to continue in the grace of God."[12] Not what we would expect! Here was a synagogue full of Jewish people warmly accepting the message of the gospel and even inviting the speaker to return the next Sabbath and speak more on the topic.

However, others were in attendance as well. As Paul began his address he said, "Brothers, sons of Abraham, and you God-fearing Gentiles, it is to us that this message of salvation has been sent."[13] The threefold address refers to the three types of people one might find in any diaspora synagogue of the first century.

1. "Brothers" are Jews: In the context of the Pisidian Antioch synagogue, Paul's brothers were his fellow Jews. He means to refer to those who are ethnically Jewish, born Jewish as physical descendants of Abraham, Isaac, and Jacob. In the first century, the word "Jew" did not specifically mean someone from the tribe of Judah. It was used as a broad designation to refer to any natural-born Israelite. Thus, Paul referred to himself as Jewish, though he was in actuality a Benjamite. The Jews, Paul's brothers, are the physical descendants of Israel.

2. "Sons of Abraham" are proselytes: The second type of congregant Paul found in the Pisidian Antioch synagogue was the proselyte. They were Gentiles who had, for one reason or another, decided to make a formal, legal conversion to Judaism. According to the legal opinion of the rabbis, Gentiles who underwent ritual conversion were no longer regarded as Gentiles. Through the rituals of circumcision and immersion (and sacrifice at the Temple when possible), they had been reborn as "Sons of Abraham." Henceforth, they had legal Jewish status.

3. "God-fearing Gentiles" are non-Jews: The third type of congregant Paul addressed that day in the Pisidian Antioch synagogue was the God-fearing Gentile. The term "God-fearing Gentiles" describes non-Jews who, for some reason or another, were attracted to Judaism. They worshipped in the synagogue with Jews and proselytes but chose not to undergo the ritual of conversion. They weren't exactly pagans anymore, but they were certainly not Jews. While they may have been tolerated in the synagogue, and even appreciated for their financial contributions to the community (as with the centurions in Luke 7 and Acts 10), they were not regarded as Jews. They did not enjoy the rights, privileges, and responsibilities of Judaism.

As Paul presented the good news of the gospel to the Pisidian Antioch synagogue, he included all three types of people in his address. He declared, "Brothers, children of Abraham, and you God-fearing Gentiles, it is to us that this message of salvation has been sent."[14] His message was well received by the Jews and proselytes of the synagogue, and they invited him to speak again the subsequent Sabbath. As it turned out, however, the God-fearing Gentiles received the message even more enthusiastically. After all, Paul had included them in the good news. Salvation had been sent to them as well as to the Jews and converts.

Paul's gospel gave the God-fearing Gentiles status in the Jewish community without requiring them to go through a legal conversion to become Jewish. According to Paul's gospel, the God-fearing Gentiles were sons of Abraham by merit of faith in Yeshua, and they could be regarded as brothers with the Jewish people. It was a provocative message. Word spread rapidly. By the time the next Sabbath arrived, "almost the whole city gathered to hear the word of the Lord."[15]

OFFENSE OF THE CROSS

Almost the whole city gathered? Is that hyperbole? The point is that the synagogue was packed—standing room only—filled with Gentiles. Not converts. Real Gentiles: *goyim*, *ethnos*, non-Jews, uncircumcised fellows, "Philistines."

From the evangelical Christian point of view, this would be a happy problem indeed. From the Jewish perspective, however, a Gentile majority in the synagogue was a serious threat to the integrity of the community's identity. Jewish identity was precarious enough in the face of Hellenist society. The mainstream culture was always chipping away at the particulars of Jewish monotheism and Torah observance. A Gentile presence almost certainly would accelerate the tendency toward assimilation. Besides, it was annoying.

Jews were, after all, the chosen people. It was their synagogue. Crowding just about every Gentile of the city into the synagogue created both a practical nuisance ("Hey, that guy's sitting in my seat!") and a theological conundrum (If everyone is God's chosen people, then being chosen loses its significance).

Luke tells us, "When the Jews saw the crowds, they were filled with jealousy and talked abusively against what Paul was saying."[16] They were filled with jealousy. They were not jealous because they had never been able to raise such large crowds. (The synagogues were not about the business of trying to bring in big numbers. They were not "evangelical" as we would understand the term.) They were not jealous that Paul and Barnabas had such appeal or that their message seemed to be so popular. They were jealous because the message of the gospel was compromising the particularity of their theology. The message of the gospel was throwing the doors of Judaism wide open to the Gentile world. The religion that had previously been a members-only club was suddenly declared open to the public, no table reservations necessary. Paul and Barnabas shrugged off the Jewish objections and continued to teach and minister to the new Gentile believers, but eventually, pressure from the Jewish community forced them out of Pisidian Antioch.

The message of the gospel itself raised no objections from the Galatian Jewish community; on the contrary, they listened eagerly and wanted to hear more. The message of Messiah's death, burial, and resurrection, and the justification and salvation available through him, sounded good to their ears. They found no offense in the cross. Those were the days before Christian polemics had galvanized Jewish resistance to the gospel. There was really nothing "un-Jewish" or objectionable about the message of salvation in Yeshua.

Not until they saw the Gentiles crowding into the synagogue did they raise their objections. Not until they realized how this "good news" compromised the exclusive character of Judaism did they reject Paul's message. To the Jewish community of Galatia, the offense of the cross was the inclusion of the Gentiles.

This was a pattern Paul would live to see repeated over and over in city after city. In Thessalonica, the same problem emerged. Popular success at the synagogue was followed by the conversion of "a large number of God-fearing Greeks and not a few prominent women. But the Jews were jealous."[17] Everywhere Paul went, Gentiles flocked to the synagogue to hear him speak. All over Asia Minor, Paul found Gentiles eager to hear the message of the gospel and Jews eager to be rid of that same message, not because of theological objections about Yeshua, but because they objected to the inclusion of Gentiles in their faith, religion, and synagogue.

When some Jewish pilgrims to Jerusalem from the congregations in Asia Minor spotted Paul in the Temple, they recognized him at once: "It's that guy!" They were the ones who accused Paul of bringing Gentiles past the dividing wall and into the court of Israel, even as he had brought Gentiles into their synagogues back home. They were the ones who instigated the riot and testified against him at his trials. They were the ones responsible for Paul's chains.

As Paul wrote the epistle to the Ephesians, the shackles were still on his wrists. He told the Ephesians that it was "the mystery of the gospel, for which I am an ambassador in chains."[18] He was a prisoner for the sake of the mystery of the gospel. But what was the mystery of the gospel to Paul? Why was he in chains? The mystery of the gospel that held Paul fast in chains was not the mystery of the death and resurrection of Messiah (though that is mysterious indeed); it was the mystery of the Gentile inclusion in Israel. To Paul, the inclusion of the Gentiles into the House of Israel was the mysterious part of the gospel.

He reminded the Ephesian Gentiles that it was for their sake he was a prisoner:

> For this reason I, Paul, the prisoner of the Messiah Yeshua for the sake of you Gentiles—Surely you have heard about the administration of God's grace that was given to me for you, that is, the mystery made known to me by revelation, as I have already written briefly. (Ephesians 3:1–3)

The mystery made known to Paul by revelation was that the gospel was for Gentiles too. The revelation by which the mystery was made known to him took place in the Temple, many years before, when the Master appeared to Paul in a vision and said to him, "Go; I will send you far away to the Gentiles."[19] Because of that mystery made known to him by revelation, Paul tells us, he was a prisoner for the sake of the Gentiles. Because of that revelation, he was in chains in Rome. He speaks further:

> In reading this, then, you will be able to understand my insight into the mystery of Messiah, which was not made known to men in other generations as it has now been revealed by the Spirit to God's holy apostles and prophets. This mystery is that through the gospel the Gentiles are heirs together with Israel, members together of one body, and sharers together in the promise in the Messiah Yeshua. (Ephesians 3:4–6)

To Paul, the mystery of Messiah is that the Gentiles are heirs together with Israel as members of one body. The Gentiles share, together with the Jews, the promise in Messiah. The Gentile inclusion is the mystery of Messiah.

Such an unanticipated turn of events, from the ethnocentric perspective of Israel, is a mystery indeed! Moreover, it was this mystery, this powerful truth, that inspired Paul's apostleship. It drove him on when all other drives failed. It was the fire that burned in his belly and forced him repeatedly into harm's way. He explains:

> I became a servant of this Gospel by the gift of God's grace given me through the working of his power. Although I am less than the least of all God's people, this grace was given me: to preach to the Gentiles the unsearchable riches of Messiah, and to make plain to everyone the administration of this mystery [i.e. the Gentile inclusion], which for ages past was kept hidden in God, who created all things. (Ephesians 3:7–9)

This is deep stuff. Paul was talking about a mystery that has been kept hidden in God for ages. It is a mystery with which Paul believed he had been entrusted. It was a secret concealed for all the ages of creation: "The Gentiles are heirs together with Israel." It is the mystery of Messiah.

2
SONS OF ABRAHAM

Genesis 12

As Paul pored over the Scriptures for confirmation of the mystery he had discovered, he must have rolled the scroll back to the story of Abraham in the book of Genesis. Father Abraham stands as a central figure in Paul's theology. Abraham, who believed God and was credited with righteousness even before circumcision, is a cornerstone of Paul's arguments for the inclusion of the Gentiles.

The story of Abraham began while he was still called Abram. It began with a promise regarding his seed and his relationship to the whole world. It began in Genesis 12 when God said to Abram:

> I will make you into a great nation
> And I will bless you.
> I will make your name great,
> And you will be a blessing.
> I will bless those who bless you,
> And whoever curses you I will curse.
> And all peoples on earth will be blessed through you.

The LORD's promises to Abram in this initial covenant oracle culminate with the last line: "All peoples on earth will be blessed through you." It is an astounding promise because of its universal scope. Through a single man, all the families of the peoples on earth will be blessed. God does not say how he intends to accomplish this. He simply assures Abram that, somehow, Abram will be the agent through which all peoples on earth will be blessed.

In its simplest reading, it would seem that we are to understand that all nations will be blessed through Abram because God has declared that he will bless those who bless Abram. Thus, all nations will be blessed through Abram to the extent that they bother to bless him. If they don't bless him, they won't be blessed through him. It turns out to be good news for Abram because it means that all nations will eventually have to bless him in order for the prophecy of their own blessing through him to be fulfilled. That's a lot of blessing going around.

As to be expected, the sages of classical Judaism were not content with the simple explanation. They saw several deeper meanings in the oracle of Genesis 12. They perceived a way in which Abraham might be a deeper blessing to all peoples.

Procreation or New Creation

The sages took it for granted that Torah is the inspired word of God and that every word of Torah is sacred. Even the smallest jot and tittle have meaning, and even the spaces between the letters are important. The sages regarded the choice of a specific word over another word as significant and intentional. Minute details of phrasing and syntax are fraught with meanings. The rabbis' exacting study of such subtle nuances gave rise to the body of interpretation we call "midrash." Midrash means "something searched out." A midrash is an interpretation that has been searched out.

The first words of God's promise to Abraham are "I will make you a great nation." Those words are loaded with enough nuance and meaning to give rise to a lot of midrash. For example, consider Reb Berekiah's interpretation.

Reb Berekiah pointed out that God did not say to Abram, "I will give you a great nation," nor did he say, "I will establish you as a great nation." Rather, it is written, "I will make you a great nation." Reb Berekiah suspected that God must have had a reason for using the verb "make" rather than any of the other verbs he could have used. God must have intended to communicate something to us by the deliberate choice of that word. Reb Berekiah suggested that God's choice of words was meant to convey that Abram would become a great nation only after he was *remade* by God. It is as if God said to Abram, "I will make you a great nation only after I have created you as a new creation. Then you will be fruitful and multiply."[20]

Reb Berekiah speculated that Abram's metamorphosis into a great nation would not be incumbent upon procreation. Had God simply meant to prosper Abram into a great nation through the means of fertility and progeny (opening wombs and closing wombs), he might have phrased this blessing otherwise. Instead, God said to Abram, "I will make you." Therefore, in Reb Berekiah's opinion, it was the spiritual rebirth of Abram as a "new creation" that was critical to the fulfillment of the promise.

Reb Berekiah's interpretation would have fit well with the Apostle Paul's theology. According to Paul, Abram received the blessings of the covenant on the merit of his faith. Moreover, on the merit of his faith, Abram was remade into Abraham, the father of many nations.[21] For Paul, the story of Abram's transformation into Abraham is the essential prototype of salvation by faith.

In the faith of Abraham, Paul finds a model for the faith of the Gentile believers. By virtue of that same faith that recreated Abram into Abraham, a father of many nations, the Gentiles were also recreated as "new creations."[22] Just as Abram, by faith, became Abraham, a new spiritual creation, so too Gentiles by faith become new creations in Messiah. According to Paul, the Gentiles who are thus recreated by God are made into sons of Abraham. "So then, [Abraham] is the father of all who believe," Paul writes in Romans 4:11.

The transformation of the believing Gentiles into sons of Abraham fulfills the "new creation" name of Abraham, "father of many [Gentiles]." Through faith in the God of Abraham, Gentiles from many nations are remade into sons of Abraham. Through the proliferation of these Gentile believers, Abraham has become a great nation, fulfilling the words of the oracle.

Paul and Reb Berekiah must have been studying from the same set of notes.

In addition to Reb Berekiah's observations about God's choice of a verb in the phrase "I will make you a great nation," the *Midrash Rabbah* goes on to make an issue out of a noun in the phrase "and you will be a *blessing*." The Hebrew word for "blessing" (*berachah*) sounds similar to the Hebrew word for "pool" (*berechah*), and so invited the sages to indulge in some wordplay. Regarding the clause "and you will be a *blessing*," the midrash says, "you will be an *immersion pool*: Just as a pool purifies the unclean, in the same way you bring near to Me those who are far away."[23]

Because the word for "blessing" and the word for "pool of water" are very similar in Hebrew, the sages played off the similar-sounding words to construe a new meaning for Abraham's blessing. According to the new meaning, Abraham is to be like a *mikvah* (baptismal pool), which Gentile converts immerse themselves in as part of the ritual conversion to become Jewish. Converts to Judaism pass through a "baptism" in a pool of living water. This immersion into a baptismal pool is the final ritual of conversion. Gentiles who pass through the immersion pool are symbolically reborn as Jews (or "born again" as Jews, if you prefer).

The issues of Gentile conversion, immersion in *mikvah*, and being born again will be subjects of a later chapter. For now, suffice it to say that the midrash is indulging in some creative wordplay. It's a metaphor. Abram is not really an immersion pool. But how else is one to describe being "baptized" into another except by means of metaphor?

Abraham's role is to bring near to God the Gentiles who were formerly far away. By performing this role of bringing the Gentiles near to God, Abraham will be a blessing to the Gentiles. As the pagans embraced the faith of Abraham, they were symbolically immersed into him, as if he were an immersion pool suitable for the conversion ritual.

The immersion ritual of conversion into Judaism brought near to God those who were formerly far away by legally changing pagan Gentiles into Jews. In Jewish law, one who immerses in the water of conversion undergoes a legal transformation. He goes down into the water a Gentile, but comes out of it as an Israelite in every regard. Previous ethnic affiliations are no longer deemed relevant.

The new convert is even marriageable for anyone in the Jewish community except for those of priestly descent.

This midrashic re-reading, wherein Abraham is likened to an immersion pool for conversion, would have suited the Apostle Paul. He used the same symbolism when he spoke of Messiah. Paul's Gentile converts were "immersed into Messiah Yeshua."[24] Paul employed language similar to that of the midrash in order to describe how the Gentiles, who were formerly far away and strangers to the covenants, were brought near to God. To the Ephesian assembly he wrote, "Remember that at that time you were separate from Messiah, excluded from citizenship in Israel, and foreigners to the covenants of the promise, without hope and without God in the world. But now in Messiah Yeshua you *who once were far away have been brought near* through the blood of Messiah."[25]

Again, it would seem that Paul was drawing his material from the same sources as the sages. He even employed the same terminology as the sages to refer to Gentiles: "[those who are] far away."

THE FIRST MISSIONARY

How can Abram be compared to an immersion pool? What possible similarity can exist between Abram and a conversion ritual? Again, we must turn to the sages. In the midrashic commentary on Abraham's life, Abraham is always depicted as busy making proselytes from the nations. His goal in life was to spread the knowledge of God and to bring all men to faith in the one God. Consider my literal translation of Genesis 12:5:

> And Abram took Sarai his wife and Lot the son of his brother and all their possessions they possessed and the souls which they had made in Haran, and they went out to go to the land of Canaan, and they came to the land of Canaan.

"The souls which they had made ..."? Normally we would smooth out the Hebrew by translating the word *souls* as "people" and the word *made* as "acquired." The sages, however, read the passage literally, and they objected that Abram and Sarai were not able to make souls. What then does the Torah mean by telling us that they made souls in Haran? The literal reading says, "the souls which they had made in Haran."

> Rav Leazar said: "It refers rather to the proselytes they had made. The verse, as it is written is to teach you that he who brings a Gentile near to God and converts him is as though he had created him."[26]

Rav Leazar's explanation of the passage is in accordance with the traditional characterization of Abraham and his relationship to Gentiles. Jewish tradition paints Abraham and Sarah as missionaries for God, actively engaged in the pursuit of the Gentiles. In this manner, Abraham was fulfilling his role as a blessing to all nations. By converting the Gentiles to faith in God, Abraham was being a blessing, and all peoples were blessed through him.

Just as an immersion pool is the means by which Gentiles convert into Judaism, Abraham was the means by which Gentiles were brought into relationship with the one true God. Just as an immersion pool brings near those who were once far away, so too Abraham was the agent that brought the pagan world to a knowledge of God.

In that sense, Abraham was the first missionary.

Blessed and Grafted

In the eyes of the sages, Abraham was to be a blessing to all nations by converting them to faith in God. In support of this view, the traditional sources raise yet another nuance of meaning in the oracle God gave to Abraham.

Genesis 12:3 says, "And all peoples on earth will be blessed through you." The Hebrew verb (*v'nivracu*) translated as "will be blessed" is related to a Mishnaic Hebrew term (*mavrich*) that means "to intermingle, to graft."[27] Thus, one might translate the verse as "All peoples on earth will be grafted into you."

The context of the passage makes this alternative reading impossible. Clearly, the Torah intends us to read, "All peoples on earth will be blessed through you." The passage has nothing to do with the grafting of plants. It is a passage about blessing and being blessed. A responsible translator would never translate the verse to read, "All peoples on earth will be grafted into you." However, the sages are seldom accused of being responsible translators. In the Talmud, we read the following:

> Rabbi Elazar expounded, "What is meant by the verse, 'And all peoples on earth will be blessed through you'? The Holy One, blessed be He, said to Abraham, 'I have two goodly shoots to engraft on you: Ruth the Moabitess and Naamah the Ammonitess.' All the families of the earth, even the other families who live on the earth are blessed only for Israel's sake. All the nations of the earth, even the ships that go from Gaul to Spain are blessed only for Israel's sake." (b. *Yavamot* 63a)

Rabbi Elazar uses the passage to explain how two Gentile women came to be regarded as part of Israel and even mothers of the Davidic kings. Ruth was a Moabite. Naamah was an Ammonite. The Torah says, "No Ammonite or Moabite or any of his descendants may enter the assembly of the LORD, even down to the tenth generation." [28] How then could Ruth and Naamah be mothers of the Kings of Israel? The answer is that they were no longer to be considered Moabite and Ammonite. They had been grafted into Abraham.

This creative re-reading of the passage is consistent with the above-cited midrashic interpretations and traditions, which portray Abraham as actively involved in missionizing the pagan world. In his efforts to turn the world to faith in God, Abraham could be likened unto a tree of faith. As people left the pagan religious systems and idolatry of the world, they are likened to branches removed from trees of other faiths. They are cut from those trees and grafted into the tree of Abraham's faith. As the peoples of the world turn to faith in the God of Abraham, they are, in a metaphorical sense, grafted into Abraham. This engrafting process is a blessing to the peoples of the earth, for only in Abraham's faith can they find truth. Thus, we may read, "All peoples on earth will be *blessed* through you" as "All peoples on earth will be *grafted* into you."

The grafting parable is Paul's, but the concept that "all peoples on earth will be grafted into you" is not his invention. Rather, it is an intentional misreading of the Hebrew. Paul and Rabbi Elazar were virtually contemporaries. Either Paul found the inspiration for his olive tree parable in the same misreading of Genesis 12:3, or Paul and Rabbi Elazar shared a common source. At any rate, Rabbi Elazar's imagery is consistent with Paul's theology.

Paul equated that very line of Hebrew text (Genesis 12:3) with the full message of the gospel. In Galatians 3:8 he quoted Genesis 12:3, saying, "The Scripture foresaw that God would justify the Gentiles by faith, and announced the gospel in advance to Abraham: 'All nations will be blessed through you.'" To Paul, the phrase "all nations will be blessed through you" is *the gospel.* In his estimation, those very words are the good news of Messiah.

The sages of the midrash and Talmud understood Abraham's blessing of all nations to be accomplished through the conversion of those nations to faith in God. This was also Paul's understanding of the Abrahamic promises. In Paul's version of the engrafting parable (Romans 11), Israel is an olive tree and the Gentile believers are olive branches, cut from other trees and grafted into the olive tree of Israel. It is a vivid illustration of the blessing of Abraham to the nations.

"All peoples on earth will be grafted into you."

THE SEED OF ABRAHAM

In Genesis 12, God also promises Abram a seed. He says to Abram, "To your [*seed*] I will give this land" (verse 7). This was news to Abram, who had no children.

In Genesis 13, God expanded upon the seed promise. He said, "I will make your [*seed*] like the dust of the earth, so that if anyone could count the dust, then your [*seed*] could be counted" (verse 16). Despite the fabulous promises, Abram continued to be childless. As the years went by, it seemed to Abram that God must have overlooked the fact that he had no children. Finally, Abram complained to God, pointing out in Genesis 15, "You have given me no [*seed*]" (verse 3). God responded by taking Abram outside on a starry night. He said, "Look up at the heavens and count the stars—if indeed you can count them. So shall your *seed* be." When God said this to Abram, "Abram believed the LORD, and he credited it to him as righteousness."[29]

God's promise to give Abraham seed was literally fulfilled with the birth of Isaac. Isaac was the seed of Abraham. Therefore, when God told Abraham to sacrifice Isaac as a burnt offering, the command tested both his devotion to God and his faith in the promises of God. When Abraham proved his faith by obeying the horrid command, the LORD rewarded him by reiterating the covenant promises and the promise of his seed. He said, "I will surely bless you and make your [seed] as numerous as the stars in the sky and as the sand on the seashore. Your [seed] will take possession of the cities of their enemies, and through your [seed] all nations on earth will be blessed, because you have obeyed me."[30] The promise that "all peoples will be blessed through you" was made specific to say, "*Through your [seed] all nations on earth will be blessed.*"

This idea is repeated in Genesis 26:4, where God passed the blessing to Isaac, saying, "Through your [seed] all nations on earth will be blessed." From Isaac the promise was passed to his seed Jacob, to whom God said in 28:14, "All the peoples on earth will be blessed through you and your [seed]."

Let's consider this for a moment. How was Abraham's seed to be the vehicle by which all nations might be blessed? How was it that through Abraham's seed all nations should come to faith? Paul responds to these questions in Galatians 3:16. In that passage, Paul points out that the "seed of Abraham" and the seed of the patriarchs is always represented in the Hebrew by the singular form of the noun. Paul says, "The promises were spoken to Abraham and to his seed. The Scripture does not say 'and to seeds,' meaning many people, but 'and to your seed,' meaning one person, who is Messiah."[31]

According to Paul, the promised seed of Abraham is not a multitude of nations, nor is it a vast sea of people. Rather, it is a singular individual by whom vast seas of people are blessed, and multitudes are recreated as seed of Abraham. For Paul, the promise of the seed finds its ultimate fulfillment in Messiah, a singular seed of Abraham. This singular seed is the agent through which all peoples and all nations are blessed (converted). Messiah is the seed through which the Gentiles are made into new creations. He is the seed through which those far off are brought near. He is the seed into which the unclean are immersed and made clean. He is the seed by which the wild olive branches are grafted into the family tree of Israel.

Through the work of the singular seed of Abraham, Gentiles from all nations have been transformed into the innumerable seed of the promise. Paul concluded his argument in Galatians when he declared to the Gentile believers, "You are all sons of God through faith in Messiah Yeshua, for all of you who were baptized into Messiah have clothed yourselves with Messiah. There is neither Jew nor Greek, slave nor free, male nor female, for you are all one in Messiah Yeshua. If you belong to Messiah, then you are Abraham's Seed, and heirs according to the promise."[32]

According to Paul, if we belong to Messiah (who is the seed of Abraham) then we are Abraham's seed and the recipients of the promise of being blessed in that seed. Paul's criteria for determining if one is indeed of the seed of Abraham is not genetic; it is spiritual. If you belong to Messiah, then you are Abraham's seed and an heir according to the promise. You are part of the greater collective of Israel. The only criterion is belonging to Messiah.

ALL PEOPLES ON EARTH WILL BE GRAFTED INTO YOU

We saw how an "alternative" reading of the Hebrew of Genesis 12:3 could be construed to read, "All peoples on earth will be grafted into you."

Paul seems to have taken his cue from the same alternative reading, but even if he did not, he came to the same conclusion. In Romans chapter 11, he compared Israel to an olive tree. Paul explained to his Gentile readers in Rome that they had been adopted into the family tree of Israel. They are adopted like wild olive branches taken from other olive trees (other nations) and grafted into the olive tree of Israel. The result of the engrafting is that they became a full part of the olive tree of Israel. They are no longer Gentiles in the strict sense. In Messiah, there is neither Jew nor Greek. Instead, both the natural and legal descendants of Abraham (Jews and proselytes) and the descendants by faith (Gentile believers) comprise the broader entity of Israel.

In this sustained metaphor for spiritual adoption, Paul warns the Gentiles not to become arrogant over the natural branches. Rather, they should remember that, as engrafted branches, they are the guests. He admits that some of the natural branches have been removed from the tree because of their unbelief. However, even this unbelief he explains away as a necessary and temporary state to allow time for the nations to come to faith.

Who are the natural branches that have been removed? The context of the book of Romans seems to make it clear that those branches are Paul's own Jewish contemporaries who have rejected the gospel. Regarding those branches, Paul tells us, "As far as the gospel is concerned, they are enemies on your account; but as far as election is concerned, they are loved on account of the patriarchs, for God's gifts and his call are irrevocable."[33] In other words, don't be too quick to count them out.

3
THE HOUSE OF JOSEPH

Genesis 45

Stories are powerful.

As Paul wrestled with the mystery of the gospel, trying to come to terms with the Gentile inclusion, he might have rolled the scroll to the stories of Joseph. In Paul's day, other voices were already retelling the stories of Joseph as metaphors for Gentile inclusion—and exclusion.

The Torah tells a story about Joseph taking a wife in Egypt. During Joseph's time of estrangement from his family, he took an Egyptian bride. Her name was Asenath. She was the daughter of a pagan priest. We are told nothing else about her except that she bore Joseph two sons: Ephraim and Manasseh. Her two sons went on to be patriarchs of two of the twelve tribes of Israel.

Joseph's Egyptian wife was something of an embarrassment to the sages. Abraham's wife, Sarah, was a Hebrew like himself. When Abraham sought a wife for his son Isaac, he sent his servant on a quest to find a girl from his own people. He wanted a Hebrew, Shemite bride for his son. Abraham's servant procured Rebecca. Isaac and Rebecca had two sons. They grieved over Esau because he took wives from among the local girls. Jacob's wives, on the other hand, were Hebrew Shemites like his mother and grandmother. But Asenath was the daughter of an Egyptian priest, and hence a Hamite. Joseph's marriage to her appears to be a breach of ethnic fealty. One can almost hear Grandma Rebecca's disapproving "tsk-tsk" echoing from inside the Machpelah tomb in Hebron.

Daughter of Dinah

The embarrassment over Asenath comes from the implication that two of the Israelite tribes had Egyptian blood in their veins from the outset. In response to this uncomfortable moment in the Torah, the sages supplied a midrashic explanation for Joseph's marriage to Asenath. According to this explanation, Asenath was Joseph's niece, the daughter of his sister Dinah. Of course Joseph did not realize this, but through miraculous circumstances, his niece had been adopted by Potiphera and raised as an Egyptian. Therefore, Asenath, the bride of Joseph, was not an Egyptian at all; she was really an Israelite in disguise. The happy result of this retelling of the story is that Ephraim and Manasseh (and hence the tribes that bear their names) are full-blooded sons of Jacob.

The midrash says, "When Shechem son of Hamor violated Dinah, she conceived and bore Asenath. Jacob's sons wished to kill the child. What did Jacob do? He inscribed the Divine Name on a gold foil, hung it about her neck, and sent her away. The angel Michael descended and brought her down to Egypt into the house of Potiphar. Potiphar's wife, being barren, raised Asenath as a daughter."[34] In the story, Jacob's gold-foil dog tag with the ineffable Name inscribed on it serves to identify her later. This assures us that she is indeed Dinah's daughter and not a horrid Egyptian woman after all.

The revision of the story is primarily concerned with the purity of bloodlines. We can imagine the sage who created this explanation for Asenath. He is a respected teacher in his community, perhaps with his own school of disciples. As the Torah authority of the local *Beit Midrash* and synagogue, he feels responsible for safeguarding the community. What's more, he is not particularly fond of proselytes.

He has seen both converts to Judaism and Christians turn against the Jewish community when the political pressure to do so was applied. He has seen the deleterious effects of Gentile worldviews in the Torah community. He has had to deal with the legal problems raised by mixed marriages. He has seen more than enough Jewish blood spilled by Gentile hands.

His disciples come to him with a question. "Master," they ask, "how is it that Joseph, who proved his purity and devotion to his father's family when tempted by the Egyptian woman, succumbed to be married to the heathen daughter of an Egyptian priest?"

The old sage considers the question. How should he answer? He might answer, "Asenath was a proselyte that converted to Judaism; thus Joseph was free to marry her." But such an answer would seem to sanction mixed marriages. It might even encourage his disciples to consider Gentile women for themselves, Heaven forbid. What would prevent one of his disciples from marrying a Gentile woman whom he had convinced to make a similar conversion? Furthermore, such an answer would imply that the tribes of Ephraim and Manasseh were not pure descendants of Shem—an unconscionable conclusion to reach. The sage understands that his telling of the story of Asenath will shape the identity of the Jewish community for better or for worse.

He considers it a moment more and answers with a question. "What of the other eleven brothers? From where did they obtain their wives?"

His disciples have no answer. This question had not previously occurred to them. From where indeed? Aside from the ill-fated marriage of Judah, the Torah does not say.

"I will tell you from whence they found wives," the sage says. "The wives of all the tribes were born along with them, from the same womb even. Each of Jacob's sons was born as a fraternal twin with his wife. Thus, God provided good Israelite wives for each of our fathers. Except for Joseph."

Now the sage has a smile on his face. He has his disciples hanging on his every word. Their mouths are agape. Their eyes are riveted on him. He chuckles as he asks, "And from where was Joseph to obtain a wife? Why did God provide an Israelite bride for each of his brothers but not for him?"

The disciples shake their heads. They do not know why.

"I'll tell you why," the sage says. "Because Dinah's daughter Asenath was fitting for him as a wife."[35] As his explanation grows, the story of Asenath's birth, her abandonment, her angelic transportation to Egypt, and her adoption by Potiphera are all supplied as necessary details to support the premise.

By imagining sibling spouses for the sons of Jacob and by reinventing Asenath as a granddaughter of Jacob, our sage has avoided the unpleasant implications of mixed bloodlines. In addition, he has protected his ethnocentric worldview, which places Gentiles outside of the people of God. Never mind that Dinah's own daughter, child of a Canaanite rape, could hardly have been of a pure bloodline herself. It is enough that the reproach of Joseph has been removed.

He has reinvented Asenath. He has made her into a symbol and confirmation of the exclusion of the Gentiles. She may at first appear to be a Gentile convert, but on closer examination, she proves to be a lost daughter of Israel. Objections to his interpretation are waved away by fanciful claims and a creative retelling of the story. Asenath must be Israelite because the alternative is unthinkable. It cannot be proven and it need not be proven, because it is a matter of identity. It is a story, not a history.

However, his fanciful retelling is contrary to the literal reading of the Torah. In the Torah's account, Asenath is Egyptian. She is the blood-daughter of an Egyptian, and Joseph marries her because he has no hope of ever being reunited with his family. His marriage to her results in two sons. Joseph names the elder Manasseh ("forgetful") because he has forgotten his father's family. He names the second son Ephraim ("doubly fruitful") because God has made him twice fruitful with two sons.

The midrash wants to adjust the plain meaning of the text in order to avoid the unpleasant implication that two of the tribes of Israel have an Egyptian mother. By trying to control the story, the midrash hopes to control Jewish identity.

DAUGHTER OF EGYPT

But there exists another, and perhaps older, answer to the question about Joseph's bride. This interpretation of the Asenath character comes from the pen of a Greek-speaking Jewish author living sometime in the first century of the common era. We don't know his name or where he came from, but we can infer some things about him from his writing. He wrote in Greek. He had an interest in things Egyptian and seemed to have firsthand knowledge of Egyptian geography. He may have been an Egyptian Jew living in Alexandria.

In his community, he had probably seen scores of Gentiles turn from their idolatrous worship systems and attach themselves to the God of Abraham. The great port city of Alexandria afforded him plenty of occasions to rub shoulders with all manner of men. He met people from all nations who had joined themselves to Israel as proselytes and converts. They were Greek speakers for the most part, but they possessed a deep passion for the God of the Hebrews. They were God fearers, converts, and Christians. They crowded themselves into the Great Synagogue; they pressed themselves in among Israel. From the Egyptian writer's perspective, the presence of those Gentiles enriched the family of God.

As a result, he took a very positive view of converts. Perhaps he himself was a convert to Judaism. In his book, *Joseph and Asenath*, his interpretation of the Asenath character is considerably friendlier toward Gentiles than that of the midrash cited above.

Joseph and Asenath is a suggestively erotic love story about Joseph and his Egyptian bride. In the story, Asenath is portrayed as a breathtakingly beautiful, virgin daughter of an Egyptian priest. Despite her great beauty, she is completely devoted to idolatry and worships all the gods of Egypt. Yet when she lays eyes on Joseph, she is so smitten that she says, "I did not know that Joseph is a son of God."[36]

She tries to woo him, but he is not interested. He rebukes her for her idolatry, and she is filled with shame. Having fallen utterly in love with Joseph, she destroys all of her idols, repents for seven days in sackcloth and ashes, and calls upon the God of Joseph. During her seven days of repentance, a heavenly man appears to her. He is described as "a man in every respect similar to Joseph … except that his face was like lightning and his eyes like sunshine and the hairs of his head like a flame of fire of a burning torch, and hands and feet like iron shining forth from a fire."[37] The heavenly Joseph-Man is similar to the Son of Man descriptions in the books of Daniel and Enoch.

The Joseph-Man speaks to Asenath, saying, "Take courage, for behold your name was written in the book of the living in heaven in the beginning of the book, as the very first of all, your name was written by my finger and it will not be erased forever. Behold, from today, you will be renewed and formed anew and made alive again and you will eat the blessed bread of life, and drink a blessed cup of immortality, and anoint yourself with blessed ointment of incorruptibility. And your name shall no longer be called Asenath, but your name shall be 'City of Refuge,' because in you many nations will take refuge with the LORD God, the Most High, and under your wings many peoples will be sheltered and behind your walls will be guarded those who attach themselves to the Most High God in the name of repentance." [38]

After her encounter with the divine Joseph-Man, Asenath converts into a worshipper of the LORD God Most High. She confesses her sins and washes herself from the ashes of her repentance. She dresses herself in a wedding garment and waits for her beloved to return.

The Pharaoh of Egypt informs her, "The LORD, the God of Joseph, has chosen you as a bride for Joseph, because he is the firstborn son of God. And you shall be called a daughter of the Most High." [39] At last, Joseph and Asenath are married, after which Asenath says to Joseph, "Your father Israel is like a father to me."

CITY OF REFUGE

Joseph and Asenath is an important work because it presents a first-century typology of both the Joseph character and the Asenath character. In the mind of the writer of *Joseph and Asenath*, Joseph represents a messianic figure. He is even called "the firstborn son of God." The divine Joseph-Man gives Asenath to eat from the "blessed bread of life" and to drink from the "blessed cup of immortality." These seem to be clear allusions to the rites of the Last Seder. Through the agency of this messianic Joseph character (who is represented as both divine and earthly) Asenath is converted from paganism to the worship of the one true God. The imagery seems pointedly Christian, and it may be that our Alexandrian Jewish author was also a believer. [40]

Unlike the midrashic explanation of Asenath, our unknown author revels in Asenath's Gentile roots and pagan origin. It is her Gentile and pagan nature that intrigues him. In her he sees a model for all future converts to Judaism. She is a "City of Refuge" for all nations and peoples who attach themselves to the Most High God.

By creating this charming story, our unknown Jewish author lends us an important alternative interpretation of the Asenath character and the Gentile question. His readership was probably composed of Gentile converts to Judaism (or the sect of Judaism called "The Way"). Asenath is offered to them as a sort of patron saint. She is the Torah matriarch for Gentiles seeking legitimacy in Israel.

In this respect, Asenath's character is a proto-Ruth. Like Ruth, Asenath is a Gentile daughter of a people forbidden to intermarry with Israel. Like Ruth, Asenath makes a dramatic declaration of conversion. Like Ruth, Asenath is ultimately brought into Israel through marriage to a Redeemer-Messiah character.

Through her attachment to Joseph, Asenath becomes the bride of a son of God and a daughter of the Most High.

WILL THE REAL ASENATH PLEASE STAND UP?

These two interpretations of Asenath are roughly contemporary. Yet they could not be more opposite in orientation. The midrashic view rises from a defensive and ethnocentric Judaism that views Gentile converts as a threat to the integrity of the Jewish race and religion. The *Joseph and Asenath* view rises from a confident and expansive Judaism that views Gentile converts as a complement to Israel and a testimony to the universal validity of faith in God.

Which view is correct? It depends on whom you ask. Neither story is historical. Rather, they are stories written to shape a people's corporate self-consciousness. Whoever controls the stories of a people controls the identity of the people.

The two versions of Asenath have striking similarities to the questions posed by many Gentile believers in Messianic Judaism today. Which Asenath better represents Messianic Gentiles? Are Gentile believers like the daughter of Dinah, lost and forgotten Israelites raised in a Gentile environment, ignorant of their own true identity as Israel, until it is revealed to them through their salvation and the teaching of the Two-House theology? Or are Gentile believers like the daughter of the Egyptian priest, a real Gentile fallen head-over-heels in love with Joseph the Israelite, forsaking pagan identity and clinging to Joseph and his God? I would opt for the latter.

The author of *Joseph and Asenath* definitely would place us in the latter camp. His messianic treatment of Joseph creates a typology into which Yeshua fits very well. As the bride of Yeshua, we are his Asenath. And like Asenath, we are brought into the family of Israel through our husband. As Asenath tells Joseph in the story, "Your father Israel is like a father to me." Asenath is a City of Refuge in Israel for those of us who have attached ourselves to the Most High God, the God of Israel.

A Prayer for Asenath

In the story *Joseph and Asenath*, Joseph prays for his beautiful Egyptian princess prior to her conversion. The prayer eloquently expresses the hope of our faith, our desire to be born again, to be remade and renewed and brought into the family of the God of Israel. Listen to the words of Joseph as he prays for his Gentile bride:

> LORD God of my father Israel
> The Most High, the Powerful One of Jacob
> Who gave life to all
> And called from the darkness to the light
> And from the error to the truth
> And from the death to the life.
>
> May you, LORD, bless this virgin,
> And renew her by your spirit,
> And form her anew by your hidden hand,
> And make her alive again by your life,
> And drink your cup of blessing,
> And number her among your people
> That you have chosen before all came into being,
> And let her enter your rest
> Which you have prepared for your chosen ones,
> And live in your eternal life forever and ever. [41]

4

JOSEPH AND HIS BROTHERS

Genesis 45

Almost a decade later, Joseph found himself face to face with his long-estranged brothers. When at last he could sustain the ruse no longer, he turned his back on his guests and servants and shouted in Egyptian, "Have everyone leave my presence!"

Only Joseph's stunned and terrified brothers were left in the room. Judah was still on his knees in front of the Egyptian governor, but the governor had turned his back. Judah let his eyes travel across the suddenly silent and abandoned hall. He looked into the wide-eyed and terror-stricken faces of his brothers.

A sound from the governor broke the silence: a small gasp, a breath, a sob. His shoulders convulsed as a deeper sob escaped from his body—and then another sob, followed by another one, rising from inside him. The governor sank to the ground, his back still turned away from the anxious brothers. His sobs broke into a wailing howl of such immense sorrow and pain that Judah felt his own eyes fill with tears.

The Egyptian governor turned toward the brothers and tried to stand, but the weight of his agonized weeping buckled his knees and he stumbled to the ground again.

The brothers stared, uncomprehending. They began to suspect that they had fallen victim to a lunatic. But this lunatic reached out his hand toward them, beckoning. Only by great force of will was he able to choke out two simple Hebrew words between his cries. He said, *"Ani Yosef."*

To the brothers, he may as well have still been speaking Egyptian, because even in their own language, the words he spoke made no more sense than if they had been Egyptian. He said, "I am Joseph! Is my father still living?"

WHO IS JOSEPH?

The scene in which Joseph reveals his identity to his brothers is the climactic moment of the book of Genesis. Everything in the narratives of Genesis builds to this point.

To truly enter into the moment, the reader must remember that at this point in the story, Joseph's brothers still have no idea who he is. Joseph is dressed like an Egyptian. He has Egyptian hair and Egyptian makeup. He speaks the Egyptian language and, until this moment, has only spoken Hebrew through a translator. To the eleven brothers, Joseph is a Gentile prince. They have no idea that this is their own brother, the one sent to them by their father so long ago, the one they rejected, stripped, put into the earth, and gave over to the Gentiles. And how could they suspect it? The brothers had long ago come to regard Joseph as dead, convincing themselves of their own deceit to explain his absence. To the brothers, there is no Joseph.

Ever since the days of the Master, his followers and believers have explained the importance of the Joseph story as a type and a foreshadowing of the story of Yeshua. Although the apostolic writers never directly invoke it, the symbolism is unavoidable and remarkably clear. The line of connection between Joseph and Yeshua of Nazareth was certainly not lost on the Christian readers of *Joseph and Asenath*. In that work, Joseph is the firstborn son of God, manifested in both a human and a divinely glorified state, offering his bride to eat from the blessed bread of life and to drink from the blessed cup of immortality.

While we read the story of Joseph, we must remind ourselves that there is another story at work here, the story behind the story, a deeper meaning, a messianic midrash. It runs parallel to the Joseph story like a second line of narrative. It is the deep mystery of Genesis. It is the story of our Master and his reconciliation with his brothers.[42]

Yeshua, like Joseph, was sent to his brothers, the people of Israel. Like Joseph, he was sent by his father. Like Joseph, his brothers did not receive him. Instead, he was rejected, stripped, killed, put into the earth, and ultimately given over to the Gentiles.

Like Joseph, Yeshua was variously received among the Gentiles, but eventually rose to an unparalleled position of prominence in the Gentile world. Like Joseph, he became the agent for the salvation of all nations. And like Joseph, he was all but forgotten by his own true brothers.

Just as Joseph was disguised—made unrecognizable by his Egyptian clothing and hairstyle—so too the Messiah has been made unrecognizable—disguised by Gentile culture. We have painted him to look like one of us. We have represented him in our artwork with Gentile hair, makeup, and clothing. We have made his mouth speak in Greek and in the language of every nation, but we have forgotten that he spoke Hebrew first. We have removed him from his Hebraic and Torah context, and made him unrecognizable to his own brothers. Historically, the harder we have tried to convince Jewish people otherwise, the more we have strengthened their conviction that Jesus is not a Jew, and he is certainly not the Jewish Messiah.

When Joseph finally chose to reveal his identity, it was in his own timing and his own venue. He cleared the room of Gentiles. There was nothing for any of the Egyptian court to contribute or to add to the moment. It was only theirs to hurry and get out of the way. So too with us from the nations. When the Master chooses to reveal himself to his brothers, it is he who does the revealing.

The great Chassidic teacher Rabbi Yisrael Meir Kagan, better known as the Chofetz Chaim, commented on this passage of Genesis. Like many others before him, he intuitively sensed the great import of the events being described as Joseph revealed his identity to his brothers. Reb Kagan wrote, "When Joseph said, 'I am Joseph,' God's master plan became clear to the brothers. They had no more questions. Everything that had happened for the last twenty-two years fell into perspective. So, too, will it be in the time to come when God will reveal himself and announce, 'I am the LORD.' The veil will be lifted from our eyes and we will comprehend everything that transpired throughout history."[43]

What more is there to say? The veil will be lifted. Messiah himself will lift the veil and reveal his identity to his brothers, saying, *"Ani Yeshua!* I am Yeshua, your brother." Then the veil will be lifted from our eyes and we will comprehend everything that transpired throughout history.

Joseph's Shadow

When Joseph revealed himself to his brothers, he said, "Come close to me … I am your brother Joseph, the one you sold into Egypt! And now, do not be distressed and do not be angry with yourselves for selling me here, because it was to save lives that God sent me ahead of you."[44]

Joseph told his brothers not to be angry or regretful over the circumstances of the past. It was God's plan that he should be estranged from them. It was God's plan to send Joseph ahead of them to save lives. So too, Israel's rejection of the Messiah has meant wealth for all nations. His rejection at the hands of his brothers is a central part of God's plan to bring salvation and resurrection to all peoples, even to his own brethren. God willed it to save lives. God sent him ahead of his brothers to save lives.

The book of Romans tells us of a hardening. Paul's second epistle to the Corinthians tells us of a veil. We live in the days that the Apostolic Scriptures call the time of the Gentiles. Paul tells us that the Jewish rejection meant "riches for the Gentiles."[45] So too with Joseph. His brothers' rejection of him was not accidental; it was necessary. It meant riches for the world, life to the dead.

Joseph continued to speak to his frightened and amazed brothers. He said, "And now, do not be distressed and do not be angry with yourselves for selling me here, because it was to save lives that God sent me ahead of you … God sent me ahead of you to preserve for you a remnant on earth and to save your lives by a great deliverance. So then, it was not you who sent me here, but God."[46] Just as Joseph was sent ahead of his brothers to preserve a remnant on earth and to save lives by a great deliverance, so too Messiah has been sent ahead of Israel to preserve a remnant and to save lives by a great deliverance.

We are not trifling with the text nor are we bending things to force the Hebrew Scriptures into the shape of Christian interpretations. The story tells itself. Joseph is a redeemer of Israel, a demonstration of how God does redemption, a portrait of what redemption looks like. The shadow cast by Joseph's character is so clearly messianic that the sages of the Talmud adopted the title "Messiah son of Joseph" to describe the suffering servant messiah prophesied in Isaiah and Zechariah. In those interpretations, the messianic office was split into two. The suffering and afflicted messiah was named Messiah son of Joseph, perhaps because his redemptive sufferings were reminiscent of the difficulties that Joseph encountered. The victorious, conquering messiah was called Messiah son of David because he was seen as the Davidic descendant coming to rule over Israel.

In the two-Messiah interpretation, the Joseph-Messiah dies in the redemption process. For example, the Talmud suggests that the passage in Zechariah 12, which says, "They will look on me, the one they have pierced, and they will mourn for him as one mourns for an only child," is a reference to the death of Messiah son of Joseph, who dies while redeeming Israel. [47]

In the Gospels, Philip the disciple introduces the Master to Nathaniel as Yeshua ben Yosef, Jesus the son of Joseph, the one Moses wrote about in the Torah, the one the prophets wrote about.

BENJAMIN

The temptation to push the analogy further is too great, and I have succumbed.

In our messianic interpretation of the Joseph story, the Joseph character symbolizes Messiah, and Joseph's eleven brothers symbolize Israel. But among the brothers is the odd character of Benjamin. Benjamin is the silent yet key player in the narrative.

Benjamin is the younger son of Rachel. He was not part of the rejection of Joseph. He was not party to the deception of Jacob. He is the brother who did not sell Joseph to the Egyptians. At the time the unpleasant incident happened, he was just a child. In fact, Benjamin seems to vanish from the narrative and to be all but forgotten until he re-emerges at the end of the story.

If the other ten brothers represent Israel's rejection of Messiah, Benjamin must represent that portion of Israel that did not reject Messiah. Perhaps this is too much for our critical sensibilities. Perhaps I have pushed the symbolic interpretation of the text too far. But if I have, be patient and at least enjoy the metaphor with me.

In the narrative, Benjamin has a place among the brothers. He is one of the sons of Israel, but he has never abandoned Joseph. In the analogy, he is believing Judaism. He represents the remnant of Israel that did not reject Messiah. In the days of the Master, Benjamin represents the disciples, the *talmidim*, the believers, the *Notzrim*, the sect of the Nazarenes, those called *HaDerech*, "The Way." Benjamin is believing Israel—the Jewish believers.

In the Genesis narrative, it is with Benjamin that Joseph hid his cup. Benjamin received five times the portion from Joseph's table. He had the cup of the Master. He ate from the table of the Master.

Benjamin could be seen as a symbol for Messianic Judaism. The Apostle Paul was a product of first-century Messianic Judaism. His amazing salvation story is a sort of paradigm for the Jewish experience with Messiah. His story involved a personal encounter with the risen Master. In a vivid dramatization of the revelation, Paul was literally blinded, and then his eyes were literally opened. His shock at the revelation of Messiah's identity was no less than the shock of Joseph's brothers in Genesis 45.

By coincidence, Paul is the only apostle to give us his tribal identity. In both Romans and Philippians Paul tells us that he is of the tribe of Benjamin. He is the paradigmatic Jewish believer and, by coincidence, a son of the tribe of Benjamin.

In the literal reading of biblical history, Benjamin is a small tribe of great consequence. At one point, the men of Benjamin became so immoral that all the other tribes turned against them. Out of Benjamin came the first king of Israel. Benjamin's strategically valuable territory contained the sacred city of Jerusalem. Benjamin was a buffer zone between the two powerful tribes of Ephraim and Judah. Ultimately Benjamin's territory was the strategic prize that the tribes battled for.

The Psalmist recognizes Benjamin's unique position. Psalm 68 creates a vision of a future day when God returns to his Temple in Jerusalem in great pomp and pageantry. Surprisingly, the little tribe of Benjamin leads the procession to the Temple.

> Your procession has come into view, O God,
> The procession of my God and King into the sanctuary.
> In front are the singers, after them the musicians;
> With them are the maidens playing tambourines.
> Praise God in the great congregation;
> Praise the LORD in the assembly of Israel.
> There is the little tribe of Benjamin, leading them,
> There the great throng of Judah's princes,
> And there the princes of Zebulun and of Naphtali.
> Summon your power, O God;
> Show us your strength, O God,
> As you have done before.
> Because of your temple at Jerusalem
> Kings will bring you gifts. (Psalm 68:24–29)

JEWISH BELIEVERS

In the Joseph narratives, Benjamin is introduced at his birth and then disappears from the story until near the end. The same is true of believing Judaism. She appeared on the scene in the days of the apostles, but quickly vanished from the record of history, only to reappear now as the story begins to culminate.

The preceding century saw the amazing fulfillment of many prophecies relating to the return of the Jewish people to the land of Israel. No less surprising than the formation of the modern state of Israel was the reappearance of believing Judaism. To be sure, throughout church history, there have always been Jewish converts. Jewish believers within Messianic Judaism, however, are different. Messianic Jews claim that they are not Jewish converts to Christianity. Rather, they are Jewish believers retaining their full Jewish identity.

Modern Messianic Judaism is an odd hybrid of religious impulses. The modern Messianic movement began as a missionary effort of the evangelical church. Who better to bring the gospel to Jews than Jewish Christians? That was the reasoning. Jewish-

Christian organizations began to reach out to the Jewish community in order to proselytize.

I remember my excitement as a young boy in small-town Minnesota when a Jewish speaker from Jews for Jesus came to our little evangelical church to speak. I had never met a real Jewish person, much less a Messianic Jew! There were no Jewish people in our part of Minnesota. What's more, we were hosting him in our house for dinner. My sister suggested we serve ham as a test of his conversion. She was joking, of course, but the theological assumption we made was that as a real Christian, he could have no qualms about eating pork.

We did not serve ham.

The idea of Jewish believers captured my heart and imagination. It was incredible. It was the most exciting thing to ever happen at my church. The idea! The possibility!

That was back in the early 1970s. Jews for Jesus was one example of the kind of Jewish outreach organizations that were actively using Jewish believers as missionaries to pursue the Jewish people for conversion to Christianity.

As part of the attempt to reach the Jewish people, these outreach missions began to imitate Judaism. The reasoning, as I see it, went something like this: "If we met on Saturday instead of Sunday, maybe Jews would feel more comfortable. If we did some synagogue liturgy instead of old hymns, maybe Jews would feel more comfortable. If we said 'Shalom' instead of 'Hello, how are you?' maybe Jews would feel more comfortable. If we say 'Yeshua' instead of 'Jesus;' if we say 'Shaul' instead of 'Paul;' etc." As a result of repackaging Christianity for Jewish consumption, a uniquely Jewish subculture began to develop within these organizations.

The original intent of the missionaries was to spread Judaism like peanut butter on a piece of bread. The bread was traditional Christianity. But now it had a Jewish flavor. At best, it was a trick. A fake. The old bait-and-switch.

Messianic Judaism began as something of a facade conceived with the intent of luring Jews into the Christian faith. In some ways, much of the facade still remains. From its inception, such an enterprise flirts with disingenuousness and invites pretense and pretending. In terms of converts, the results have been underwhelming.

However, as a result of these missionary efforts, something unexpected happened. The expected result was that Jewish people would pour into the Christian faith. What happened was something completely unintended. In the attempt to create an artificial Judaism, the Jewish missionary movement hit upon something authentic: Torah.

When Messianic Judaism decided to meet on Shabbat so that Jewish people would feel more comfortable, someone must have raised the obvious question, "Hey, isn't this the real biblical Shabbat anyway?" And when Messianic Judaism started doing the festivals to make Jewish people interested, someone must have pointed out, "These festivals teach about Messiah. This stuff is all about Messiah!"

Messianic Judaism had accidentally stumbled into Torah. The rediscovery of Torah promises to be the most enduring contribution to the faith that Messianic Judaism will make. What began as a ruse emerged as a reality. Believing Judaism has spawned small communities of Torah. Today, Jewish believers are meeting in their own synagogues and congregations all over the world, living out Torah lives and retaining Jewish identity.

The world has not seen congregations of Jewish believers living Torah lives in obedience to the Master for almost two thousand years. Like Benjamin reentering the Joseph story at the end of the narrative, believing Judaism has returned.

If the effectiveness of the Messianic Jewish movement was to be weighed in terms of how many Jewish people have been evangelized, we would have to say that, so far, it has been less than a fabulous success. But if we weigh the effectiveness of the movement in terms of how it has begun to restore Torah to the body of Messiah, the results are impressive. It has drawn disenfranchised Jews back to their own heritage, back to Torah and to Messiah, and it has revealed to us the authentic, first-century pattern of our faith. In those terms of measurement, Messianic Judaism has been a wild success. And it has just begun.

In the Torah, Joseph refused to reveal his identity to his brothers until Benjamin was brought before him. Messianic Judaism may yet have an important role to play in the revelation of the identity of Messiah. However, if Messianic Jews are to play this role, they must be true to their own identity. Messianic Judaism must not pretend to be Jewish; rather, it must live out Judaism as an authentic component of faith in the Jewish Messiah.

Messianic Gentiles?

Another surprising and unanticipated result of the Messianic Jewish movement is the Gentile Christian response to the Torah mode of life and worship. Anyone around the Messianic Jewish movement is quick to observe the disproportionate numbers of non-Jews crowding into the Messianic synagogues. Oftentimes, when visiting a Messianic Jewish synagogue, one detects a distinct lack of Jews.

Ironically, the Messianic Jewish movement is becoming a largely Gentile phenomenon. Oftentimes, those who look the most Jewish (dressed in Jewish garb and such) are not Jews at all.

This is one of the strange things that gives the Messianic movement a surreal quality. If you went to a Russian Orthodox Church, you might expect the people to be of Eastern European descent. If you went to an Ethiopian Coptic church, you'd expect most of the people to be Ethiopian. You would likely find Coptic Christians who weren't Ethiopian, but you certainly wouldn't expect to meet a Norwegian from Wisconsin who was pretending to be an Ethiopian.

Gentiles have been joining themselves to the Messianic Jewish movement for years. A lot of Gentile believers don't understand why they feel compelled to worship and live in a Torah mode. They are not sure why they are drawn to Jewish expression. They do not necessarily feel like they fit in within Messianic Judaism, but they do not fit within the mainstream church any longer either. They feel that their short exposure to the Hebrew roots of Christian faith has been enough to ruin them in relation to their original churches. But where is there room for Gentiles in a religion defined by an ethnicity they do not share?

On the other hand, it is not unusual for Jewish believers to become frustrated with the Gentiles filling the seats of their synagogues. Many Jewish believers within the Messianic movement joined the Messianic synagogue because they were unhappy being the "token Jew" within a Christian church. Now they look around the synagogue and realize that they are again the "token Jews" in a congregation of non-Jews. At other times, Jewish believers have protested that the Gentile presence in their congregations serves as a deterrent to effective Jewish evangelism. Messianic Jews often object to Gentiles keeping Torah and doing Jewish things, because it blurs the distinction between Israel and the nations.

For these reasons, even though the Messianic Gentiles may constitute a majority in some Messianic Jewish congregations, they are less than welcome. They might be met with resentment from the leadership and sometimes open hostility. They are told that the Jewish mode of life does not apply to them.

The result for these bewildered Gentiles is a problem of identity. We aren't Jewish, but we often look like, worship like, and live like observant Jewish people. So what are we? We are hard-pressed to explain our passion for Torah and Judaism.

This sense of identity crisis sends some of us searching back through our genealogical records, trying to find a Jewish ancestor. We are searching our family trees, looking back through our old records for Jewish-sounding names. "I must have a Jewish ancestor a few generations back. How else can I justify attending a Messianic synagogue?"

But even if I can prove that I have a Jewish ancestor, does that somehow validate me? If I have a Jewish great-grandfather, am I therefore Jewish? Not according to Judaism. According to the legal determination of Jewishness, that simply makes me a Gentile with a Jewish great-grandfather. It may be of sentimental value to me, but it does not make me Jewish.

We find ourselves looking for some kind of validation for our presence in the Messianic community. If we cannot find a valid reason to explain ourselves and our identity, we are left with the uncomfortable possibility that we are merely posers and Jewish wannabes.

Posers and Wannabes

The Gentile presence within the Messianic movement is another unwitting result of Jewish evangelism's accidental rediscovery of Torah. In the attempt to create an artificial Judaism, Messianic Judaism rediscovered an authenticity deeper and older than the modern church: Torah. Instead of Jewish people coming into the

Messianic synagogue, the Messianic movement began to attract Christians—Gentile Christians starved for authenticity and seeking biblical foundations, Gentile Christians hungry and zealous for Torah.

This was an accident. But when Messianic Judaism began to return to Torah in order to create a more Jewish venue, it struck a chord deep within the hearts of many Christians: "Yes! This is what my faith has been missing. This is what I have been looking for."

Gentile Christians within Messianic Judaism do not want to be regarded as posers or wannabes. But most of us would rather accept that denigration than let go of what we have discovered.

Not everyone in the Hebrew Roots movement is willing to be a poser, though. On the other side is the Christian who is too authentic to pretend to be something he or she is not. I once heard a Christian teacher speak for an hour about the Sabbath and all the wealth of riches that the Torah life offers to Judaism. He was enthralled with the Jewish mode and regarded it as the truly biblical walk of faith, but he concluded his lecture sadly. He said, "We Christians will always be on the outside, looking in."

Vast numbers of Christians long for the things of Torah but feel they cannot possess them, because those things are only for Jews. We are on the outside, looking in at Torah and the practice of Judaism, like pauper children pressing their noses to the window of a toy store. Our eyes are wide with excitement, but we know that we can never possess the things we see.

For Christians in this camp it is acceptable to read about and study Judaism and Torah, but it is not acceptable to cross the line and begin to practice those things. To do so, we fear, would be legalism and Judaizing. Instead, we must go on with our regular church traditions and Christian practice. Of course, we would love to do Sabbath; our hearts leap at the thought. But the Sabbath is for Jews and we are Gentiles. Of course, we would love to live a Torah life, but we are Gentile Christians, and Gentile Christians are not under the Law. So we must stay on our side of the glass. It's all right to look, but not to touch.

Those seem to be the only two options for Gentiles. We must either pretend and fake it or stay on the outside and look in longingly. But could there be a third way—a third option?

5
THE SONS OF JOSEPH

Genesis 48

The old patriarch is dying. It won't be long. Joseph and his two sons have come to bid him farewell. The rest of Joseph's brothers have come too. They are all old men now with gray hair and beards themselves. They are grandfathers and even great-grandfathers. They are all assembled outside of the tent, waiting to be called. They hope to receive their father's blessing as he departs from the world, even as he received the blessing from his father, Isaac, who in turn received it from his father, Abraham.

Joseph is called into the tent.

The many years of hardship and heartbreak have worn on Jacob. He looks frail and thin as he lifts himself from his bed. A servant admits Joseph into his presence.

Out of respect for his father, Joseph stands quietly, waiting for his father to break the silence. Jacob begins to deliver the words he has been rehearsing in his mind. He says to Joseph, "God Almighty appeared to me at Luz in the land of Canaan, and there he blessed me and said to me, 'I am going to make you fruitful and will increase your numbers. I will make you a community of nations, and I will give this land as an everlasting possession to your seed after you.'"[48]

Joseph nods. This is not new information for him. This is a reiteration of the covenant promises given to his great-grandfather Abraham, then to his grandfather Isaac, and finally to his father,

Jacob. But why is his father telling him this? Does his father mean to pass this blessing on to him? Does his father intend to skip over his brothers, as Abraham had passed over Ishmael, as Isaac had passed over Esau? Is Joseph to be the sole inheritor of the promise of the seed?

But Jacob has something else in mind. He continues speaking to his son, saying, "Now then, your two sons born to you in Egypt before I came to you here will be reckoned as mine; Ephraim and Manasseh will be mine, just as Reuben and Simeon are mine."[49]

It takes a moment for it to sink in, but when it does, Joseph smiles. He understands. His father, Jacob, intends to adopt his sons. By adopting Joseph's two sons, Ephraim and Manasseh, Jacob will elevate those boys to a station of headship equal to the rest of his sons. Ephraim and Manasseh will become brothers of the twelve sons of Jacob. The two sons will double Joseph's standing among his brothers. When Jacob's inheritance is divided among his sons, Ephraim and Manasseh will each receive a portion equal with that of the other brothers. The adoption maneuver results in Jacob's bestowing a double portion of his inheritance upon the house of Joseph. The double portion is the right of the firstborn. Even though Joseph is not actually the firstborn among the brothers, Jacob intends to ensure that he be accorded the honor regardless.

Jacob's adoption of Joseph's two sons will also result in making Joseph's sons his siblings. Thus, Joseph will become a "brother" of Ephraim and Manasseh.

Jacob goes on to explain his reason for bestowing this firstborn right upon Joseph. A shadow passes over his foggy eyes as he says, "While I was returning from Paddan, to my sorrow Rachel died in the land of Canaan while we were still on the way, a little distance from Ephrath. So I buried her there beside the road to Ephrath."[50] Joseph is Jacob's firstborn son through Rachel. Rachel was Jacob's first love and the only wife he ever intended to marry. In Jacob's mind, Joseph is the true firstborn. As a token of his affection for Rachel, he intends to accord the honor of firstborn to her son Joseph by adopting Ephraim and Manasseh as his own children.

Ephraim and Manasseh enter the tent of their grandfather. Their names mean "fruitfulness" and "forgetfulness," respectively. They are young men. As they stand before the old patriarch and their father, Joseph, they fidget nervously and shift their weight from foot to foot. They look more like Egyptians than like Hebrews. Their mother is the daughter of an Egyptian priest. They are dressed in the garments of the Egyptian court. Their hair is shaved in the Egyptian style. It is hardly any wonder that Jacob, with his failing eyes, says, "Who are these?"

Their grandfather does not recognize them. For a moment, they must feel that they surely do not belong in this tent or among this strange family of their father. But Joseph answers, saying, "They are the sons God has given me here." With a genuine note of delight in his voice Jacob says, "Bring them to me so I may bless them."[51]

Jacob wraps his frail old arms around Ephraim and kisses him. He embraces Manasseh and kisses him. The boys are visibly relieved to receive such a warm welcome from their grandfather. "I never expected to see your face again, and now God has allowed me to see your children too," Jacob says.[52]

Then, in keeping with the ancient ritual of adoption, Jacob sits the boys on his lap. It is an awkward and comical shuffling about as the big teenagers find themselves being seated on the knees of this fragile old man. This is the ancient ritual by which adoptions are made official, and rituals are usually a little awkward. As Joseph helps remove his sons from Jacob's knees, he realizes that they are no longer his sons. Instead, they are his brothers. In a gesture of gratitude, he bows down before Jacob with his face to the ground.

Now that Ephraim and Manasseh are his own sons, Jacob intends to give them the blessing of sons. He reaches out his hands to place them on the heads of the boys, but as he does so, he crosses his arms and places his right hand on Ephraim's head, though he is the younger, and he places his left hand on Manasseh's head, even though Manasseh is the firstborn. Jacob takes a deep, rasping breath and draws the spirit of prophecy into his lungs. Then he begins to bless the house of Joseph, saying, "May the God before whom my fathers Abraham and Isaac walked, the God who has been my shepherd all my life to this day, the Angel who has delivered me from all harm—may he bless these boys. May they be called by my name and the names of my fathers Abraham and Isaac, and may they increase greatly upon the earth."[53]

When Joseph realizes that his father has placed his right hand on the head of Ephraim, the second-born, he says, "No, my father, this one is the firstborn; put your right hand on his head." Joseph takes hold of Jacob's right hand to try to gently move it from Ephraim's head to Manasseh's head.

However, Jacob's inversion of the birth order is not accidental. He says, "I know, my son, I know. Manasseh too will become a people, and he too will become great. Nevertheless, his younger brother will be greater than he, and his seed will become a fullness of nations."[54]

Jacob knows that they will indeed be blessed. So abundant will be the blessing he has placed upon them that their names will become synonymous with blessing. He laughs out loud and says to his new sons, "In your name will Israel pronounce this blessing: 'May God make you like Ephraim and Manasseh.'"[55]

Fathers still bless their sons with those words even to this day. Every Shabbat the father of the home lays his hands upon his sons and pronounces this blessing over them: "May God make you like Ephraim and Manasseh."

But what does it mean to be like Ephraim and Manasseh?

Like Ephraim and Manasseh

During his time of estrangement from his family, Joseph took Asenath, an Egyptian bride. Through her, Joseph bore two sons, Ephraim and Manasseh. The two sons of Joseph and Asenath went on to become patriarchs of two of the twelve tribes of Israel.

Ephraim and Manasseh were the sons of an Egyptian mother. They were raised in the Egyptian court. Aside from a common faith in the God of their father, Joseph, they seemed to have no identity among the sons of Israel. They were grandsons, not sons. By appearances, Ephraim and Manasseh were Gentiles, raised in a Gentile environment.

It was not until Jacob deliberately adopted Ephraim and Manasseh as sons that they received their identity as sons of Israel whereby they could take a direct share of the inheritance. When Jacob took the boys upon his knees in the rite of adoption, the ritual accomplished more than just giving a double portion of the inheritance to the house of Joseph. Subsequent to the adoption maneuver, Ephraim and Manasseh were accorded full status as sons of Israel. Their previous identities became irrelevant. Henceforth they were full-blooded sons of Israel regardless of their genealogical descent. They were no longer sons of Joseph and Asenath. They were sons of Israel.

Ephraim and Manasseh were not considered stepsons of Jacob, nor were they regarded as grandsons of Jacob. Rather, they became sons. The Torah, of course, is not concerned with their Egyptian half-breed status because paternity determines identity. But subsequent to the adoption, neither their previous maternity nor paternity had any further bearing on their status. They became full sons of Jacob. That is the result of the absolute power accorded to biblical adoptions.

Who Are Ephraim and Manasseh?

Joseph represents Messiah. His brothers represent the Jewish people. Benjamin represents Jewish believers. Who are Ephraim and Manasseh?

Jacob himself poses the same question when he first sees the two sons enter his tent. He says, "Who are these?" [56] The Torah means for us to ask the same question. Who are they? Manasseh and Ephraim are the sons born to Joseph in those years while he was estranged from his brothers. They are Manasseh and Ephraim, "Forgetfulness" and "Fruitfulness." They are children raised in Gentile Egypt, sons of Joseph's Gentile bride.

In the extended analogy I am spinning, they are Gentile Christians: non-Jewish believers. They are the followers of Jesus. They are those born in the years while Messiah is estranged from his brothers. They are called "Forgetfulness" and "Fruitfulness." We Gentiles may have forgotten the house of Jacob, but we have been fruitful. We are like the children raised in Egypt. During our long estrangement from the house of Jacob, we have maintained a faith in the God of Abraham, Isaac, and Jacob. Our faith was transmitted to us through Yeshua, just as Ephraim and Manasseh maintained faith in the God of Abraham only through the testimony of their father, Joseph. Like Ephraim and Manasseh, we have been complete strangers to Jacob and the sons of Israel.

But now, through the firstborn rights conferred upon Messiah, the only begotten of the Father, an amazing reversal of fortune has befallen us. Jacob took Ephraim and Manasseh on his knees in the rite of adoption. So too, we have been adopted into the commonwealth of Israel. Like Ephraim and Manasseh, we are no longer to be regarded as foreigners to Israel but as fellow citizens.[57] Like Ephraim and Manasseh, we are adopted sons.[58] Like Ephraim and Manasseh, we have received full rights as sons.[59] Like Ephraim and Manasseh, we have become heirs together with Israel.[60] Like Ephraim and Manasseh, we have been grafted into the family tree of Israel.[61] Just as Ephraim and Manasseh were raised to the level of brethren with Joseph, so too we have been raised to the level of brothers with Messiah.[62] This is our spiritual inheritance.

This theology is radically different from what Christianity has historically taught. Historically, we have believed and taught a theology of replacement and substitution by which the church has replaced and even superseded Israel. We have believed that the church is the new Israel. We have taught that if Jews want any inheritance in the covenants, they must forsake Judaism and convert to Christianity. This is not the Torah picture.

According to our midrash on the story of Ephraim and Manasseh, it is not Israel that is joined to the church; it is the church that has been joined to Israel. Gentile Christians are adopted into Israel with the rights of sonship. We are adopted into Israel, not vice versa. Moreover, because the biblical adoption is absolute, we have real standing in the commonwealth of Israel. We are not second-class citizens. We are not stepsons or even grandsons. We are as much a genuine part of the family as are the Jewish people and legal converts to Judaism. After all, Paul tells us, even the natural-born Israelite is an adopted child, adopted by God.[63]

This does not mean that Gentile believers are Jewish. But it does mean that we have as much a place in Israel as our Jewish brothers. It means that we have a right to celebrate the Sabbath. It is part of our inheritance in Israel. We have a right to keep the festivals. They are part of our inheritance in Israel. We have a right to follow the Torah. It is part of our inheritance in Israel. We have a right to say, "Abraham our father," "Isaac our father," "Jacob our father," because we have been joined to the family of Israel.

The good news for Messianic Gentiles within Messianic Judaism is that we no longer should feel compelled to find that elusive Jew in our genealogy. We don't need to find some external validation for our participation in the community of Torah. The inheritance is already ours. We don't need to pose. We don't need to feel like pretenders. We have full participation.

To be a genuine part of Israel, we don't need to tell Yiddish jokes, eat gefilte fish, or wear a yarmulke. (Although I recommend the fish; it's not too bad.) Our position is guaranteed in Messiah. Our role is to grab hold of the fringes of his garment. He gives us standing among the tribes of Israel.

The Seed of Ephraim

Is it possible that Paul, in the process of his research, made any of these spurious connections? He was certainly familiar with rabbinic methodologies and midrashic retellings. For example, his treatment of Sarah and Hagar in Galatians 4 is merely a reworking of an old rabbinic midrash on Sarah and Isaac. Paul was not above allegorical reinterpretation. But it hardly seems likely that Paul, during his reading of the stories, would have crawled out on an allegorical limb as far as I have—were it not for one small detail. As Jacob blessed his newly adopted sons, Ephraim and Manasseh, he declared over Ephraim, "His seed will become a fullness of nations."[64]

We have already seen how Paul interpreted the seed promises of Abraham to refer to Messiah, the singular seed of Abraham. Paul went on to posit, "If you belong to Messiah, then you are Abraham's seed."[65] Seeing how the patriarchal seed promises were so fundamental to Pauline theology, it would be surprising if he had not paused to consider the implication of Jacob's words: "His seed will become a fullness of nations."

In Romans 11 Paul compared Israel to an olive tree. He explained to his Gentile readers in Rome that they had been adopted into the family tree of Israel. They were adopted like wild olive branches taken from other olive trees (other nations) and grafted into the olive tree of Israel. The result of the engrafting was that they became a full part of the olive tree of Israel. They were no longer Gentiles in the strict sense, but instead had become heirs with Israel.

Paul warned the Gentiles not to become arrogant over the natural branches. Rather, they should remember that as engrafted branches, they were the guests. He admitted that some of the natural branches (Jewish people) had been removed from the tree because of their unbelief. But even this unbelief he explains away as a necessary and temporary state to allow time for the nations to come to faith.

In Romans 11:25 he summarized this thought by saying, "I do not want you to be ignorant of this mystery, brothers, so that you may not be conceited: Israel has experienced a hardening in part until the fullness of the Gentiles has come in."

"Fullness of the Gentiles" is the phrase that Jacob used to bless his newly adopted son Ephraim. Jacob said to Ephraim, "Your seed will be a fullness of the Gentiles (nations)."[66]

By invoking Ephraim's "fullness of the Gentiles," Paul perhaps means to infer that the Gentile believers adopted into Israel are to be regarded—in a midrashic sense—as the seed of Ephraim, a fullness of the Gentiles (nations) and the ultimate extension of the Abrahamic seed promises.

Like Ephraim the son of Joseph, who was himself adopted by Israel, the Gentile believers are Messiah the son of Joseph's Gentile progeny, adopted into Israel.[67] The Gentile believers are part of the fullness of nations.

6
THE EXODUS

Exodus 14

"In every generation it is one's duty to regard himself as though he personally had gone out of Egypt, as it is written [in Exodus 13:8], 'You shall tell your son on that day: "It was because of this that the LORD did for me when I went out of Egypt."' It was not only our fathers whom the Holy One redeemed from slavery; we, too, were redeemed with them."

On the eve of Passover, at every Passover Seder meal, those words are recited from the Passover Haggadah. In a similar way, the Master himself commands all of his disciples (in every generation) to do Passover in remembrance of him. Passover and the Feast of Unleavened Bread are the "this" that he referred to when he said, "Do *this* in remembrance of me."[68]

But can a Gentile legitimately participate in the Passover?[69] This question must have occurred to Paul as he worked out the details of the mystery of the gospel. He wrote to the mixed congregations of Jewish and Gentile believers in Corinth: "For Messiah, our Passover lamb, has been sacrificed. Therefore let us keep the festival."[70]

For at least the duration of this chapter, let's fulfill the Haggadah's mandate and imagine ourselves as if we personally had gone out of Egypt. Whether you are Jewish or not, imagine that you and I are part of the exodus together. We, personally, have gone out of Egypt.

From our earliest memories, we recall the stories our father told us, late at night, after the sun had set and our eyes were growing heavy as we were falling asleep. He told us about how we are all the sons and daughters of one father, a man named Abraham. He told us how it had come to pass that in days long, long ago, Abraham our father had made a covenant with a God, the LORD. Our father told us how this strange God had made promises to Abraham, and what strange promises they were! "All nations will be blessed; your seed will inherit this land." A distant land. A promised land. And our father told us how this God had said to Abraham, "Know for certain that your descendants will be enslaved and oppressed four hundred years. But I will judge the nation whom they will serve, and afterward they will come out with many possessions."[71]

There were more stories. He told us the stories of Isaac and the stories of Jacob. He told us of Joseph and how we first came to be in Egypt. We learned of Joseph's wife, an Egyptian princess. Imagine it: us—the sons and daughters of royalty! And by the dim lamplight in the deep Egyptian nights he whispered to us the last words of Joseph: "God will surely take care of you and bring you up from this land to the land which he promised on oath to Abraham, to Isaac, and to Jacob."[72] These are our stories. This is our heritage.

Yet there were other stories. Stories of how the previous Pharaoh sought to destroy us. Casting babies into the Nile. The hard oppression. The bitterness of slavery. The infants cemented alive into the brickwork of Egypt. The stories of our fathers and the God of our fathers seemed very much removed from the reality of our daily lives.

When Moses came to us with a message from the LORD, the God of Abraham, we were skeptical. When Moses said, "This is what the LORD says: 'I will bring you out from under the burdens of the Egyptians, and I will deliver you from their bondage. I will also redeem you with an outstretched arm and with great judgments. Then I will take you for my people, and I will be your God; and you shall know that I am the LORD your God, who brought you out from under the burdens of the Egyptians,'"[73] we were more than a little skeptical.

We had heard of the LORD. We had cried out to him; we had called to him; we had longed for him; we had even worshipped him from afar—a God we had never seen. He was a God of long ago, a distant and remote God. The God of Abraham. But there were other gods in Egypt too: gods that we could see, gods that we could touch. The Egyptian gods were everywhere, all around us. They required no great leap of faith. We had built their temples with our own hands. And then, of course, there is Pharaoh, allegedly a god, a man, but a god on earth, an immortal clothed in mortal flesh.

Contest of the Gods

Despite what Moses might think he heard God say, the fact is that we belong to Pharaoh; we are Pharaoh's people. Moses tells us we will be the people of God, but we are not God's people, and he, in day-to-day reality, is not our God. We are Pharaoh's people, and like it or not, Pharaoh has exalted himself over us; he is our god. The gods of Egypt are our gods because they dominate us. It is not a matter of choice on our part. It is not a matter of faith or conviction. We are property. We are owned. If what Moses is saying turns out to be true, there will have to be a showdown, a contest of the gods.

The battle lines were drawn up like a chess game. Moses played the role of the LORD, opposite Pharaoh, who played the role of the Egyptian god. Aaron played the role of the prophet of God, manifesting the power of the LORD opposite the magicians of Egypt, who manifested the powers of the Egyptian deities.

At the first, Pharaoh had never heard of the LORD. He said to Moses and Aaron, "Who is the LORD that I should obey his voice to let Israel go? I do not know the LORD, and besides, I will not let Israel go."[74] To Pharaoh, the god-king of the world's mightiest nation, Moses and Aaron were an insult. How dare some obscure Hebrew deity make a claim on his people? His slaves! Imagine the audacity of Moses and Aaron suggesting that Pharaoh, god-king of Egypt, respect the wishes of the deity of his slaves. Pharaoh replied, "Who is the LORD that I, Pharaoh, should obey him? I've never even heard of him!"

But it was not Pharaoh alone who needed convincing. We Hebrews were ready and willing to admit to the existence of the

LORD, but the question for us was, "Will this old fairy-tale God of our fathers really be able to stand up to the gods of superpower Egypt, the most powerful nation in the world?"

He was able to stand and, in fear and trembling, we saw his glory revealed. Through the course of the ten plagues, we saw him strike down the gods of Egypt. The Egyptian pantheon was supposed to be in control of the forces of nature. There was a god of the Nile, but the Nile turned to blood. The goddess of fruitfulness, symbolized by the frog totem, was mocked with a plague of frogs. The sun god, chief of the Egyptian pantheon, was blotted out in the plague of darkness. Then, in the final plague, the slaying of the firstborn, the man-god Pharaoh himself was shown to be powerless, when his firstborn son (also a man-god) was found dead.

Remember Passover? The terrible urgency. The slaughtering knife. The lamb. We dipped the hyssop, smeared the blood; children stood watching. Through the night, we waited. Our belongings were packed. We ate a hasty meal: lamb, unleavened bread, bitter herbs. We were waiting for death. We were waiting for deliverance.

The night wore on while the full moon passed over the waters and monuments of Egypt. We listened to the silence. Our cloaks were tucked into our belts. Our staffs were in hand. Suddenly a sound, a scream rising in the night. Another cry, another shout, wailing. Terror in the night, death wandering the streets of Egypt. Then the word came to us, and we left.

God's Reputation

As individuals in the middle of this unfolding drama, concerned only with our own little lives, our own personal redemption, and our own personal salvation, we might not see the bigger picture of what is happening around us. We might not stop to ask ourselves, "Why should God Almighty care to redeem us from Egypt anyway? We've done nothing to merit his grace and favor. And why should he do it in this manner, causing pain and suffering to the Egyptians? Why the plagues? Why the gratuitous display of power?" Though we, as mere escaping slaves, might not have the wherewithal to ask these questions, God answers the questions anyway. It is a matter of reputation. His reputation.

The exodus from Egypt was God's opportunity to "declare his Name." He used the redemption of Israel to establish his reputation. Consider the following Scriptures pulled from the exodus narrative. Each one is offered by God as his rationalization behind the plagues on Egypt and the deliverance of Israel.

- The Egyptians will know I am the LORD. (Exodus 7:5)
- That you many know there is no one like the LORD our God. (Exodus 8:10)
- So that you will know that I, the LORD, am in this land. (Exodus 8:22)
- In order to show you my power and in order to proclaim my name through all the earth. (Exodus 9:16)
- That you may tell your children and grandchildren … that you may know I am the LORD. (Exodus 10:2)
- Against all the gods of Egypt I will execute judgments—I am the LORD. (Exodus 12:12)
- I will be honored through Pharaoh and all his army, and the Egyptians will know that I am the LORD. (Exodus 14:4)

Why did God do all this? Why the big display of power? Why the contest? Why did he redeem Israel? In order to show his power and in order to proclaim his Name through all the earth.

For the LORD, the contest of the gods is a demonstration of his sovereignty. Through the events of the exodus story, God is establishing his Name in the earth. He is making his entrance onto the stage of world history. In redeeming Israel, God is sending a clear message to the whole world, "I exist, I am God, there is none like me!" He is sending a message to the false gods of the world. He is demonstrating that he alone is God, and there is none other.

We are his trophies. Our redemption from Egypt serves his purpose, which is the establishment of his Name. We are part of something much bigger than just getting out of making bricks; we are part of a plan to reveal God's eternal glory to "gods" and men. We are to be like trophies of victory in the banquet hall of the King.

However, none of these grand theological notions is likely to occur to us as we leave Egypt. Our only thought is our personal salvation. For the moment, it is hard to see the bigger picture.

THE CAMP BY THE SEA

Even after the slaying of the firstborn of Egypt and Pharaoh's consent to let us go, the contest of the gods has not yet been finally decided. Moses and Aaron had asked only that we be allowed to leave to celebrate a three-day festival to the LORD. We still belong to Pharaoh. He has given us leave to stretch our legs, and that's all.

We have arrived at the shore of the Red Sea. We are setting up tents, lighting cooking fires, and preparing to settle in for the night. Animals are braying, children are running about, dodging their mothers. Our young men are taking their first taste of freedom; the old ones are smiling to themselves. The day is beginning to fade, and we are tired after our journey. The waters of the sea are to the east; the wilderness of Egypt is to the west. Looming above our heads is the strange and awe-inspiring pillar of cloud.

We are a vast number of people, a mixed multitude.[75] Pharaoh wasn't partial to Hebrews. He took slaves from all nations. The camp of Israel now includes the tents of many nations. Many peoples toiled among the slave camps of Pharaoh; many saw the light in the midst of the plague of darkness. There are many among us (I myself, for example) who saw how God had differentiated between the Egyptians and the Israelites. When we saw the Israelites marking their doorways with blood, we took refuge with them under the same blood. We are those who have left Egypt with Israel, and now we have set up our tents in the midst of their camp.

Pharaoh, however, makes no distinction between the Hebrews and the non-Hebrews. We are all slaves to him.

As the sun sets on Egypt, we look back toward the land from which we have come. As we look into the reddening western sky, we see what at first appears to be smoke. Is Egypt burning? Perhaps the LORD has poured out fire on it as he did to Sodom after Lot left. But as we peer into the sunset, it seems that the smoke is coming closer. Perhaps it is not smoke. Perhaps it is a sandstorm, a mighty wind blowing out of Egypt.

Mothers take the children into their arms. Men stop driving tent stakes and lift their eyes to see this strange sight. A feeling of uneasiness spreads through the camp.

Then we hear a low rumbling. At first, it is like the sound of distant thunder. But unlike thunder, it is sustained and seems to come up from the ground. Slowly we realize this is not smoke; it is not wind; it is the dust being kicked up from Pharaoh's horses and chariots. Even now, we can see the silhouettes of his horses and chariots coming out of the sunset. "As Pharaoh drew near, the sons of Israel looked, and behold, the Egyptians were marching after them, and they became very frightened; so the sons of Israel cried out to the LORD."[76]

Panic spreads through the camp. There is no place to run to. There is no escape. Death pursues us; death is in front of us. Women are shrieking; men are cursing. A baby is crying. Miriam, the sister of Moses, lets her tambourine slip from her hand. By now, the sound of hooves pounding the desert floor and the shouts of the charioteers are clear. Pharaoh—our god—is coming for us.

At this point, we cry out to Moses, "Is it because there were no graves in Egypt that you have taken us away to die in the wilderness?"[77] This Red Sea experience is about death and dying. In front of us is the sea. If we try to escape through it, we will drown and die. Behind us are the Egyptians. If we face the Egyptians, we will die.

IMMERSION AND CONVERSION

As Paul wrote to the mixed multitude at Corinth (a congregation of Jewish and Gentile believers who were proving to be no less a headache for him than the exodus generation had been for Moses), he made a passing comment about this passage of Torah. He said, "I do not want you to be unaware, brethren, that our fathers were all under the cloud and all passed through the sea; and all were immersed into Moses in the cloud and in the sea" (1 Corinthians 10:1).

Paul refers to the generation that left Egypt as the "fathers" of the Corinthian believers. He regards the Corinthian believers, both Jews and Gentiles, as children of Israel.

He goes on to compare the crossing of the sea to immersion. Christians generally have different ideas about how baptism should be done, but what might surprise us all is that baptism was not originally a Christian ritual. It was a Jewish ritual. From the days of Moses, immersion (baptism) was regularly practiced by all of Israel. Anyone who became ritually unclean needed to undergo an immersion before they could enter the Temple. The priests immersed every day. After a woman completed menstruation, she needed to immerse herself before she could rejoin her husband. Those who had become contaminated in any way (i.e., lepers) needed to go through immersion before they were deemed ritually pure again. In Judaism, immersions like this are referred to as immersion into a "*mikvah.*" *Mikvah* is a Hebrew word meaning "gathering of water." A *mikvah* could be a river, a lake, a spring, or any naturally fed gathering of water. Immersion in a *mikvah* was a regular part of Jewish life.

All worshippers going up to the Temple were required to first immerse themselves. Modern-day visitors to Jerusalem can see the remains of the ritual baths at the foot of the Temple steps and throughout the southern wall excavations. They are a regular feature of Jewish archaeological sites. There are immersion baths on Masada, at the Herodian, at Qumran, and all over the land of Israel. It was forbidden to come into the presence of God within his Temple without first passing through a *mikvah*.

According to Judaism, a Gentile who wants to become Jewish through conversion must undergo several ritual requirements. For men, the two main requirements are circumcision and immersion. For a woman, immersion is the entire conversion ritual. In Jewish thought, a Gentile who converts to Judaism is still a Gentile until he comes up out of the water of the *mikvah*. Going down into the water, the convert is said to die to his old life. As he comes up, he is as a newborn child, a new creature.

Born Again

The term "born again" was not coined in the early 1970s when it began to appear on American bumper stickers, nor was it invented by Yeshua or the writers of the Apostolic Scriptures. Rather, it was a rabbinic term for a Gentile who underwent a formal conversion to Judaism. In the Talmud, this concept is expressed in tractate *Yevamot*:

> When he comes up after his immersion, he is deemed an Israelite in all respects. (b. *Yevamot* 47b)

> Rabbi Yose said, "One who has become a proselyte is like a child newly born." (b. *Yevamot* 48b)

Judaism regards emerging from the *mikvah* as a symbolic rebirth. The *mikvah* represents the womb. Going into the *mikvah* is like reentering the womb, entering the place of God's creative power. Emerging from the water of the *mikvah* is like being born again. It represents a change in status.

Immersion in a *mikvah* also represents death and resurrection. Just as a person cannot breathe under water, and so enters a death-like state while under the water, a person entering the *mikvah* is like a person entering the grave. When he comes up out of the water, he comes back to life. Just as the *mikvah* represents the grave, Jewish tradition holds that a *mikvah* must be built directly into the ground.[78]

"Like one reborn" is a general Talmudic way of speaking about proselytes. The rebirth of Gentiles who passed through the *mikvah* was taken literally by the sages. Gentiles born again as Jews were regarded as having no kin. In a legal sense, they were regarded as completely new creatures. Old family ties and relations were considered defunct, as if the convert had actually died and then come back to life as a different person.

Understanding that the term "born again" originally referred to a Gentile who had undergone conversion to Judaism clears up a difficult passage from the book of John. In John 3, Yeshua and the famous sage Nicodemus[79] engaged in conversation about being "born again."

Nicodemus puzzled, "How can a man be born when he is old? He cannot enter a second time into his mother's womb and be born, can he?" (John 3:4). According to our traditional understanding of the passage, Nicodemus, a sage of the Sanhedrin, was baffled by Yeshua's use of figurative language. Rather thickheaded, wouldn't you say?

Understood from a Jewish reading, the phrase "born again" referred to a Gentile who had converted to Judaism. It referred to the symbolic death and rebirth the convert underwent as he passed through the waters of baptism. When Nicodemus objects and says, "How can a man be born when he is old?" it is not because the figurative language has left him baffled. Rather, he is employing the same metaphorical terminology that Yeshua was using. According to that imagery, Nicodemus was objecting by saying, "I am already Jewish. How can I convert to Judaism?"

Yeshua answers, "A man must be born of water and spirit." In other words, Yeshua tells Nicodemus that it is not enough to simply be Jewish. To be ethnically Jewish or even to be a convert to Judaism is not adequate for entrance to the kingdom of heaven. A spiritual conversion of the heart is the conversion experience that is really necessary. In essence, Yeshua is warning Nicodemus not to rely on his ethnicity (that is, his Jewishness) for salvation. "You need to have a converted heart," Yeshua tells him.

Dead and Alive

Paul understood the death-and-rebirth imagery of the immersion ritual as well. He applied the ritual's imagery to believers in a very similar manner. He compared the conversion rite of a believer's immersion to the death and resurrection of Yeshua:

> Do you not know that all of us who have been immersed into Messiah Yeshua have been immersed into his death? Therefore, we have been buried with him through immersion into death, so that as Messiah was raised from the dead through the glory of the Father, so we too might walk in newness of life. For if we have become united with him in the likeness of his death, certainly we shall also be in the likeness of his resurrection. (Romans 6:3–5)

Paul was invoking the rubrics of the conversion ceremony to teach us about the transformation that occurs when we place faith in Messiah. When a Gentile undergoes a conversion ritual to become legally Jewish, the Gentile is said to die to his old life and identity. In a similar way, Paul tells us that as we place faith in Messiah, we actually die to our old lives and identities. Just as in the conversion ritual, the proselyte coming up out of the water of immersion is regarded as a new creature, so too we who are immersed into Yeshua are to be regarded as new creatures, walking in newness of life. What is the newness of life? It is the resurrected Messiah within us.

Thanks to this mystical immersion into Messiah, we are reborn with a completely new identity. We are no longer who we used to be. We are no longer the old person. That identity is legally dead.

The sages of the Talmud explained, "When the proselyte comes up after his immersion he is deemed to be an Israelite in all respects."[80] Our immersion into Messiah transforms us as well— not a transformation of ethnicity, but a transformation of spirit. We are transformed into the image of Messiah. We are remade, reborn, and recreated in the living water of Yeshua. As we emerge, our lives are totally different. They must be totally different.

Perhaps we don't always feel totally different. It is likely that the average Greek converting to Judaism did not feel very Jewish as he stepped out of the water of immersion either. But legally, according to the rabbinic standard, he was henceforth a Jew. It might take that Greek a while to learn to live up to his new identity, but he was "deemed an Israelite in all respects" regardless of how he felt about it.

This isn't to say that Paul was advocating legal conversion to Judaism for Gentile believers. Far from it. We will see in later chapters that legal conversion was the very ritual against which Paul was arguing. Rather, he appropriated its symbolism and applied it to all who were immersed into faith in Messiah.

The conversion ritual is only a legal conversion. It is not magical. The Irishman who passes through the waters of conversion to Judaism is nothing more than a wet Irishman with a legal responsibility to behave like a Jew.

The immersion into Messiah, however, is more than a legal change of status. By God's standard, the Irishman who has immersed himself into faith in Messiah is no longer just an Irishman. He has the resurrected life of Yeshua; he is a whole new creature. His entire life is different. He has a new identity, a new nature, a new purpose, and a new destiny. The old man is no more. He is remade and made alive. He is born again.

When writing to the believers in Corinth, Paul compared the crossing of the Red Sea to immersion. The Israelites were all under the cloud and all passed through the sea. They were all immersed into Moses in the cloud and in the sea.

Deeper into the Water

That night, by the light of the burning pillar, Moses lifts his hand over the sea. From across the water comes a cool breeze. A shiver through the spine. The breeze grows to a gentle wind, and still it strengthens. Ripples form on the water, etching out the lines of a path across the surface. There is an excited murmuring among the people, and the wind increases. It soon becomes difficult to stand against the wind. It feels as if the very breath of God is blasting across the water. Waves are crashing. Miriam picks up her tambourine. Abruptly shooting across the water like the wake behind a sailing boat comes a line, a mark of division. With a roar like many waterfalls, the water splits to the left and to the right. It mounts and climbs, frothing and spraying, churning and splashing until it has formed a passage. It comes to rest, a wall of water on the left and a wall of water on the right.

The thousands and thousands of the host of Israel descend into the sea to walk upon the dry bottom. All night we are crossing, for we are a great and numerous people, a mixed multitude. We go with our wives and husbands, our children, our pack animals, our livestock. All that is and all that will be Israel pass through this ritual of immersion. We have descended into the *mikvah*, leaving behind forever our former lives of slavery and idol worship in Egypt. We are being baptized. We arise on the other side as free men, new creatures, every one of us born again.

Pharaoh tries to follow. The final round in the contest of the gods comes just before the first light of dawn. By the time the Egyptians realize that they cannot fight against the LORD, it is too late. They turn to flee just as the first rays of the sun spill over the eastern horizon. The waters crash over them. As the sun rises, we are a nation of free men and women standing on the shore of the sea. From our mouths, a mighty shout rises up to heaven.

The contest is over. God has made his point. He has established his reputation. There is none like him. We sing, "Who is like you among the gods, O LORD? Who is like you, majestic in holiness, awesome in praises, working wonders?"[81] In the book of Deuteronomy, Moses sums up the entire exodus episode:

> Has any god ever tried to take for himself one nation out of another nation, by testings, by miraculous signs and wonders, by war, by a mighty hand and an outstretched arm, or by great and awesome deeds, like all the things the LORD your God did for you in Egypt before your very eyes? You were shown these things so that you might know that the LORD is God; besides him there is no other. (Deuteronomy 4:34–35)

As a result of these great and awesome deeds, we stand on the opposite shore of the sea as a free people, a redeemed people. We are his people. The mixed multitude that went up from Egypt has been reborn as a free nation. We have all passed through the same immersion.

Fourteen hundred years or so later, the life of Yeshua brought yet another round in the contest of the gods. Just as God sent Moses to work signs and wonders in order to bring the Israelites out of Egypt, Yeshua was sent with the same mission. God had sent Moses as a champion, a sort of incarnation to challenge Pharaoh. He made Moses "like God" to Pharaoh. Similarly, he sent Yeshua, the true incarnation, to work signs and wonders in order to draw the hearts of the people to God. In Egypt, a lamb was slain and its blood applied to the doorposts in order that the people chosen might be saved from the last plague, the final judgment. In the same way, on Passover fourteen hundred years later, Yeshua died and his spilled blood was applied as a mark and an atonement in order that the people might be saved from final judgment. And just as the final redemption of Israel did not occur until they went down into the sea and came back up on the other side, our final redemption requires us to first be immersed into the death and resurrection of Yeshua for eternal life.

In Romans 6, Paul likened our immersion into Messiah to a death and rebirth, borrowing heavily from the rubrics of the rabbinic conversion ritual via immersion. In 1 Corinthians 10, he compared Israel's passing through the Red Sea to an immersion ritual.

This is narrative theology at work. To Paul, our salvation in Yeshua is comparable to the exodus of Israel from Egypt. Our re-creation in Messiah is comparable to Israel's passing through the Red Sea. However, Paul is not introducing anything that the Master had not taught already. It was Yeshua who compared the transformation of spirit to the experience of being born again. It was Yeshua who told his disciples to celebrate Passover in remembrance of him.

Believers are to keep the Passover in remembrance of this second and greater redemption.

This may work well for Jewish believers, but can Gentiles legitimately celebrate a Passover Seder? Can a Gentile "regard himself as though he personally had gone out of Egypt"? It would be foolish to imagine that the Master meant only for his Jewish disciples to keep the feast. Surely he did not mean for the Gentile disciples to be excluded from the table. As Paul addressed the mixed multitude in Corinth, he assumed that they were indeed keeping Passover.[82] After all, both Jew and Gentile had passed through the same great salvation. As Nicodemus learned, even Jewish people need to be born again in spirit. We need not be born again in the legal sense of a conversion to Judaism, but in the sense of rebirth in Messiah. In Messiah, we have all experienced an exodus from Egypt. All of us have passed through the sea.

We are no longer the same. Everything is different now.

7
THE FLOCK OF ISRAEL

John 10

Some stories are so powerful that they seem to breathe a life of their own. They appear and reappear in different places and in different disguises. One such story is the famous midrash about Moses the shepherd. It reads as follows:

> Moses our teacher, peace be upon him, was tending the flock of Jethro in the wilderness when a little kid escaped from him. He ran after it until it reached a shady place … and the kid stopped to drink. When Moses approached it, he said, "I did not know you ran away because of thirst, you must be weary." So he placed the kid on his shoulder and walked away. Thereupon God said: "Because you have mercy in leading the flock of a mortal, you will surely tend my flock, Israel." (*Shemot Rabbah* 2:2)

Over and over again, the Bible compares Israel to a flock. She is the flock of the LORD. Her leaders are her shepherds, appointed by her ultimate shepherd, the LORD himself. "You led your people like a flock by the hand of Moses and Aaron,"[83] the psalmist sings. "Hear us, O Shepherd of Israel, you who lead Joseph like a flock."[84]

Her greatest leaders were shepherds. Abraham, Isaac, and Jacob were men with flocks. Jacob worked as a shepherd for Laban. Moses was a shepherd for Jethro. David was shepherd over his father's flocks. It is only appropriate then that the Messiah of Israel should refer to himself as "the good shepherd."

Yeshua retells the story of Moses and the lost sheep as a parable.[85] In the parable, he casts himself in the role of Moses, seeking out the lost sheep of Israel. At one point in the Gospels, Yeshua even says, "I was sent only to the lost sheep of Israel." [86] In the realm of Two-House theology, teachers commonly explain that the lost sheep represent the lost tribes of Israel and that Gentile believers are those lost tribes. Let's take a closer look at the parables and see if this interpretation has merit.

THREE PARABLES

In Luke 15 Yeshua casts himself as the shepherd who leaves the flock of ninety-nine sheep to pursue the one lost sheep and return it to the flock. He offers the story to us as one in a series of three thematically linked parables. They are the parable of the lost sheep (Luke 15:1–7), the parable of the lost coins (Luke 15:8–10), and the parable of the prodigal son (Luke 15:11–32).

Each of the three parables is linked by a common story, theme, and meaning. The lost sheep corresponds to the lost coin and to the prodigal son. The shepherd who pursues the lost sheep corresponds to the woman searching for the coin and to the father waiting for his son's return. The ninety-nine other sheep correspond to the nine other coins and to the loyal but jealous son who did not leave home.

Yeshua told the three parables of Luke 15 in response to a criticism raised in the first verses of the chapter. He was criticized by the sages for eating with, associating with, and even teaching "tax collectors and sinners." The sages charge that Yeshua is guilty by association. If he eats with sinners and fellowships with sinners and chooses sinners for his disciples, then he must be a sinner! It is an accusation that is leveled at the Master several times throughout the Gospels, and it is an understandable point of contention.

All through his ministry Yeshua seemed to aim sharp criticisms at the religious and the faithful while generously offering warmth, hospitality, and gentle teaching to the irreligious and lawless of society. To the religious and observant Jews of the Master's day, it must have seemed as if Yeshua spurned those who strove to live lives according to God's instruction while, at the same time, he coddled those who lived in open rebellion to God. He was a friend to tax collectors, harlots, and sinners.

The Pharisees were at a loss to explain his seemingly irrational behavior. Here was a man who claimed to be a prophet of God and more than a prophet, but rather than rebuking the sinners, he rebuked the righteous!

On one occasion (Luke 5), Yeshua attempted to explain his dualistic approach to ministry. He said, "It is not the healthy who need a doctor, but the sick. I have not come to call the righteous but sinners to repentance."[87] We should not read sarcasm into the Master's words. He genuinely meant what he said. He was not interested in the religious and righteous of Israel because, by comparison to the "sinners" of his day, they were not in need of repentance. He was concerned with the irreligious. He had not come to seek the righteous, but sinners.

This explains why Yeshua was sharply critical of the religious of his day. He regarded them as the healthy and the righteous of Israel. Therefore, he held them to a much higher standard and was quick to point out hypocrisy and pretense. His criticisms, however, were not a rejection of the religious, rather, they were corrections.

On the other hand, when he was among the irreligious, he did not rebuke them as he did the Pharisees and teachers of Torah. The irreligious were outside of the domain of Torah. It does no good to rebuke someone for disobeying a law that they do not believe in. Therefore, he sought to first entice them to repent and return to obedience to the Father. He needed to bring them into the kingdom before holding them up to the standards of the kingdom.

The Pharisees and teachers of the Torah interpreted this behavior as hostility to them and love for lawlessness. Therefore, they criticized him, saying, "He hangs out with bad company." This is the situation to which the parable triplet of Luke 15 is addressed.

LOST SHEEP, COINS, AND SONS

In Luke 15 we read, "Now the tax collectors and 'sinners' were all gathering around to hear him. But the Pharisees and the teachers of the law muttered, 'This man welcomes sinners and eats with them.'"[88]

Yeshua attempted to explain his mission to seek and save the lost of Israel by retelling the famous story of Moses seeking after the lost sheep. The Master told the story this way: He said, "Suppose one of you has a hundred sheep and loses one of them. Does he not leave the ninety-nine in the open country and go after the lost sheep until he finds it? And when he finds it, he joyfully puts it on his shoulders and goes home. Then he calls his friends and neighbors together and says, 'Rejoice with me; I have found my lost sheep.' I tell you that in the same way there will be more rejoicing in heaven over one sinner who repents than over ninety-nine righteous persons who do not need to repent."[89]

In the parable, the lost sheep of Israel are symbolic of the "sinners and tax collectors." The context makes that obvious. Yeshua is the shepherd like Moses. The ninety-nine remaining sheep are the righteous of Israel who do not need to repent (present company of Pharisees and teachers of the Torah included). Yeshua explained that just as the shepherd left the flock in order to pursue and rescue the one lost sheep, so too he was leaving the religious and observant in order to pursue and rescue the irreligious and lawless of Israel.

In Luke 15, he goes on to tell the parable of the lost coins and then the parable of the prodigal son. The main point of the three parables is the same; they are explanations of why the Master was seeking after the lost of Israel.

The prodigal son represents the "sinners and tax collectors." The faithful son represents the Torah observant and religious of Israel. The father who goes to meet the prodigal and then prepares a banquet for him represents Yeshua, who was pursuing the irreligious and lawless of Israel. He told the parable to characterize the bitter attitude of the Pharisees and the teachers of the Torah toward those who were turning to repentance. They were jealous, just like the loyal son, because the Master seemed to disregard them and spend all of his attention on people of ill repute.

Each of these parables concludes with a scene of rejoicing. If there was any doubt about the meaning of the parables, Yeshua makes the meaning explicit in Luke 15:7 when he says, "I tell you that in the same way there is more rejoicing in heaven over one sinner who repents than over ninety-nine righteous persons who do not need to repent."

Lost Jews or Lost Gentiles?

Parables are not oracles. A parable is told to make a point clear and comprehensible. Parables are meant as illustrations and should be read as such. They are not allegories with multiple applications. They are told to make a singular point.

The lost sheep, the lost coin, and the prodigal son all represented Jews who had strayed from the covenant norms and were regarded by the religious of their day as "sinners and tax collectors." In fact, they *were* sinners and tax collectors, but they were still Jews.

The Master himself described his ministry in these terms. When Zacchaeus the tax collector repented, Yeshua said, "Today salvation has come to this house, because this man, too, is a son of Abraham. For the Son of Man came to seek and to save what was lost."

When he sent his disciples out to preach the kingdom of heaven in Matthew 10, he said, "Do not go among the Gentiles or enter any town of the Samaritans. Go rather to the lost sheep of Israel."[90]

When Yeshua was approached by a Gentile woman in Matthew 15, he refused to speak to her. His disciples entreated him to do something about her situation, but he replied, "I was sent only to the lost sheep of Israel."[91] In the Master's estimation, a Gentile woman does not qualify as being a "lost sheep of Israel."

The lost sheep of Israel that Yeshua sought were clearly not Gentiles or even to be found among the Gentiles. They were not the ten lost tribes. They were the sinners and the tax collectors, the backsliders, and the irreligious of the Master's countrymen. They were the Jewish people. Yeshua came to seek and save sinners. Jewish sinners.

Where does that leave us Gentile sinners?

Second-Class Citizens

When Yeshua says things like, "Do not go among the Gentiles, but only to the lost sheep of Israel," and when he says things such as, "I was sent only to the lost sheep of Israel," we Gentile followers of Yeshua are left feeling a little bit insecure. It seems as if the Master had no interest in us or as if we are second-class citizens in the kingdom. It is disturbing to think that if we had been alive in the Master's day, he may have passed us by on the basis that we were Gentiles.

Therefore, it might be very attractive to imagine that we are actually not Gentiles, but the long lost descendants of Israel—indeed, the very lost sheep of Israel that Yeshua came to seek and save. Or perhaps we may consider making a formal conversion to Judaism so that we could have legal status in that special flock of the LORD. If we are actually Israelites, then we are in the spotlight of the Gospels and at the center of the Master's concern and attention. We would be able to regard ourselves as first-class citizens.

Moreover, if we could discover that we were actually Jewish, or Israelite, or make a conversion to Judaism, then we would no longer feel awkward or hesitant about our participation in Messianic Judaism. We would no longer question our desire to live a Torah life. We would not feel self-conscious about wearing a prayer shawl or a yarmulke or affixing a mezuzah to our door, because we would be Gentiles no more. Rather, we would be the lost sheep of Israel coming home.

A Place at the Table

While it is true that the Master focused on his expressed intent to seek and save the lost sheep of Israel, he was often confronted with Gentiles vying for his attention. Ultimately, he always met the Gentile's request.

The first instance of Yeshua encountering a Gentile in need is the story of the centurion with the sick and dying servant. The episode is set in Capernaum. In the story, a certain Roman centurion heard of Yeshua and entreated the elders of the synagogue to go and appeal to him on behalf of his dying servant. The elders came to Yeshua and said, "This man deserves to have you do this, because he loves our nation and has built our synagogue."[92]

Like many non-Jews in Messianic Judaism today, the centurion had a heart for Israel and the Jewish people. The elders testified, "He loves our nation." Surely this was a man with a "Jewish heart."

He was involved in the synagogue and had been drawn to things Jewish. He probably had a mezuzah on his door.

Yeshua complied with the request of the elders and set out for the centurion's house. Before he arrived, the centurion sent word and said, "Master, don't trouble yourself, for I do not deserve to have you come under my roof."[93] The man was probably aware of the purity issues involved with Jews entering the house of a Gentile.[94] Rather than inconvenience the Master, he told him, "But say the word, and my servant will be healed."[95]

Yeshua was so impressed with the man's demonstration of faith that he said, "I tell you, I have not found such great faith even in Israel."[96] He was impressed with the faith of a Gentile.

Matthew's version of the story continues with Yeshua saying, "I say to you that many will come from the east and the west and will take their places at the feast with Abraham, Isaac, and Jacob in the kingdom of heaven. But the subjects of the kingdom will be thrown outside, into the darkness, where there will be weeping and gnashing of teeth."[97]

In this saying, the many who will come from the east and the west are Gentiles like the centurion. He and his faith are contrasted against the faithlessness of Israel. Those who come to be seated are Gentiles. Those who are cast out are Israelites.

This is a hard saying because it seems to play into the hand of replacement theology. However, it does not mean that all Israel will be rejected and replaced by Gentiles. The banquet prophecy is close to Paul's olive tree analogy. In that passage, some branches are broken off so that wild branches may be grafted in. So too with the feast in the age to come. Some unworthy elements of Israel are sent from the table in order to make room for worthy Gentiles to sit down.

In a rabbinic context, Yeshua's words are shocking. The feast with Abraham, Isaac, and Jacob is a well-known fixture in Jewish eschatology. However, in that eschatology, it is always Israel seated at the table with the patriarchs, while the Gentiles are described as the wicked. They are envisioned outside of paradise, hungry and in torment. In Yeshua's version of the story, the criterion for sitting at the table is faith, not ethnicity.

Being seated at the table with Abraham, Isaac, and Jacob is not second-class citizenship. The Master regarded Gentiles as legitimate citizens in the kingdom of heaven, seated at the table of the righteous, even seated with the patriarchs! To be seated with the fathers, one must be part of the family. Those Gentiles brought from the east and the west were not Israel, but they were seated with Israel and thus have become a part of Israel.

When Yeshua said this, he assigned Gentiles of faith the highest possible honor accorded to anyone in the whole of the kingdom of heaven. From his perspective, there is no cause for a Gentile inferiority complex. The Gentiles of faith will sit at the table of Abraham, Isaac, and Jacob—the table of Israel—together with Israel.

This saying also explains the Master's ambiguity toward Gentiles and his passion for the "lost sheep of Israel." Because he foresaw the Gentile inclusion in Israel that was coming, he was all the more passionate for the sinners and tax collectors among his own people lest they be sent from the table, thrown outside the kingdom and into outer darkness. The picture of Yeshua in the Gospels is the picture of a man on a rescue mission. He holds no disdain for Gentiles; rather he is racing against time for the souls of his own people.

Regarding those sent from the table, Paul reminds us, "And if they do not persist in unbelief, they will be grafted in, for God is able to graft them in again." [98] There is no lack of seating at God's table.

One Flock of Israel

In the parables of John chapter 10, Yeshua further illustrates his concept of the Gentile inclusion in Israel. In these passages, he returns to the flock metaphors employed in the Synoptic Gospels. Again, he is the shepherd and Israel is the flock. He speaks of guarding the flock, leading the flock, and even laying his life down for the flock. He was speaking of his relationship to his people Israel.

But then in John 10:16, he introduces sheep from another flock. He says, "I have other sheep that are not of this sheep pen. I must bring them also. They too will listen to my voice, and there shall be one flock and one shepherd."

In the John passage, the sheep being gathered and joined to the already existing flock under one shepherd are Gentiles. Notice that they are not of the flock of Israel. They are "not of this sheep pen." Sheep that are not part of the flock of Israel and not from the sheep pen (the land) of Israel are Gentiles. This is good news for Gentiles looking for a place among Israel. Notice that the Master does not say, "There shall be two flocks." Rather, there will be one flock. And it is the Gentiles who are joined to the flock of Israel, not vice versa. In the parable, Yeshua leads the Gentiles into the flock of Israel. Again, the Master does not assign Gentiles second-place status, nor does he separate them from Israelites. They are all to be in one flock, with one shepherd. The Gentiles have full participation in the flock of Israel because the Good Shepherd joins them to the flock of Israel.

The Master did not have an anti-Gentile bias. From the beginning of his ministry, he was speaking of Gentiles of faith coming into the kingdom and being seated at the table with Abraham, Isaac, and Jacob. By saying this, he assigned them a place with the righteous of Israel. In every encounter he had with Gentiles, he complied with their requests. He envisioned a day when he would lead the Gentiles like a flock of sheep and join them to the flock of Israel. From the Master's perspective, Gentiles of faith are to be identified with Israel and in Israel.

It is no surprise, then, that when Yeshua delivered the great commission to his disciples he told them, "Go and make disciples of all nations (Gentiles), baptizing them in the name of the Father and of the Son and of the Holy Spirit, and teaching them to obey everything I have commanded you."[99]

The Great Commission

During the term of his ministry, the Master focused his efforts and the efforts of his disciples on "the lost sheep of Israel." This was an urgent rescue mission, an attempt to restore the lawless of Israel (those who had strayed from Torah) to a saving faith before the doors of the kingdom would be opened to the Gentiles. At the completion of his ministry and just prior to his ascension, he lifted the ban on teaching the gospel to Gentiles. He told his disciples, "Go and make disciples of all nations (Gentiles), immersing them in the name of the Father and of the Son and of the Holy Spirit, and teaching them to obey everything I have commanded you."[100]

Oftentimes, we Gentiles in Messianic Judaism are left wondering if we really have a right to practice Judaism. We are sometimes told that the Shabbat, the festivals, the laws of kosher, and all the things of Torah are really meant for the Jews. By observing Torah and practicing the commandments, it seems we are co-opting someone else's culture. This feeling of discomfort compels us to find some rationalization for our love of Torah and our desire to keep the commandments. Either we are Jewish, Two-House tribesmen, or we need to convert to become legally Jewish.

But why should we look for validation outside of the Master?

The commandment to immerse the nations evokes the traditional conversion ritual. As we have learned in previous chapters, when a Gentile (that is, one from the nations) wants to convert to Judaism, he must pass through a ritual immersion. Subsequent to his immersion, he is regarded as an Israelite in every respect, and he is required to live a life obedient to the laws of Torah. Yeshua takes the same model and adopts it for his purposes. He commands his disciples to immerse the nations in his Name. Just as Paul later co-opted the rubrics of the conversion baptism to describe the new creation that results from faith in Messiah, the Master co-opted the very ritual itself and commanded his disciples to immerse the nations into his Name. There is a conversion implied here. It is not a legal conversion whereby one is legally transformed from a Gentile into a Jew, but a no less stunning conversion takes place as we enter the flock of the Good Shepherd.

In traditional Judaism, the proselyte is required to live a life obedient to the laws of Torah subsequent to his immersion. Yeshua told his disciples, "Immerse them … teaching them to obey everything I have commanded you."[101] Those are his words and his only instructions for us non-Jews. We are to obey everything that he commanded his disciples because we are to be disciples too. Our immersion into Yeshua is a conversion of sorts. It does not make us Jewish, but it does make us disciples. Jew or Gentile, Israelite or not, discipleship to Yeshua is our highest calling.

One of the things that the Master commanded his disciples to do was to keep the commandments of Torah.[102] We Gentile disciples will do well to obey his command. We need look no further for an explanation of our desire to walk according to Torah. We need seek no other justification for keeping Sabbath or the festivals or the kosher laws or any of the commands of Torah. We are disciples of Yeshua just as Peter, Andrew, James, and John were. Discipleship implies imitation. It is our job as disciples to imitate Messiah, and part of the imitation of Messiah is following the Torah.

The Torah is for all of Israel. Even for the Gentiles grafted into Israel.

In 1 Peter 2:25, the disciple Peter wrote to his Gentile readers, saying, "For you were like sheep going astray, but now you have returned to the Shepherd and Overseer of your souls." The Shepherd and Overseer of our souls so loved us that he left the other ninety-nine, picked us each up individually, and carried us to his flock, joining us to his flock Israel.

There is only one flock. There is only one Shepherd.

8
VOICES IN THE THUNDER

Exodus 19, Acts 2

To be Israel is to be chosen. To imply that people outside of the chosen people are also chosen is confusing. If Gentiles are made joint heirs with Israel, does this not make the Gentiles also chosen? It was one of the things that Paul needed to sort through in his investigation of the mystery of the gospel. To consider the matter, Paul must have rolled the scroll forward to Exodus 19, the story of how Israel became God's chosen people.

It happened at Mount Sinai. The sages of Israel refer to Exodus 19 as the betrothal at Sinai. The picture is a simple one. The people of Israel are the object of God's affection. He is the suitor, asking for her hand in marriage. He is to be their God. They are to be his people.

The romance actually began in Egypt. The LORD had declared to Israel, "I will take you for my people, and I will be your God." [103] The expression "You will be my people and I will be your God" is close to a legal formula from the sphere of marriage. In marriages of the ancient Near East, the groom declared, "You will be my wife and I will be your husband." In a sense, it is as if God declared his intention to marry the people of Israel.

Moses brought them out of Egypt and to Mount Sinai for the big wedding. Moses, in his role as liaison between God and the people, is sometimes described as the "friend of the bridegroom." [104] In ancient Jewish wedding custom, the friend of the bridegroom was the intermediary between the couple. It was the friend's job to present the bride to the groom. Moses filled this role by leading the people to Mount Sinai and conducting the negotiations between God and Israel. When at last the LORD descended on Mount Sinai, Moses led the people out of the camp and to the foot of the mountain, presenting them to God.

The giving of the Law at Mount Sinai is described in Jewish literature as a betrothal and a wedding. Within the midrash there are several short parables that develop this theme. They all follow the same basic construction: A princess (Israel) is captured by bandits (Egypt). A king (God) happens along, sees the princess in distress, and rescues her. He then takes her to his palace (Mount Sinai) and asks her to marry him. That's the basic layout of the imagery. There are variations. In one passage, Mount Sinai is compared to a wedding canopy. In another, the two stone tablets are referred to as the wedding contract.

If we might anthropomorphize the Holy One, blessed be he, the scene can best be illustrated as if God were on one knee before the young girl Israel, taking her hand in his, locking his eyes with hers, and imploring her, "Will you marry me?"

Here's how God posed the question:

> You yourselves have seen what I did to Egypt,
> And how I carried you on eagles' wings
> And brought you to myself.
> Now if you will really hear my voice
> And keep my covenant,
> Then out of all nations you will be my treasured possession.
> Although the whole earth is mine,
> You will be for me a kingdom of priests and a holy nation.
> (Exodus 19:4–6)

Israel responded, "We will do everything the LORD has said."[105]

The girl said yes, and the engagement ring was placed on her finger.

In actuality, getting engaged was not quite as simple as I am drawing it here. In the ancient Near East, the betrothal of a woman was a formal affair. It entailed written contract agreements in which the terms and conditions were stated. The contracts spelled out the responsibilities of both parties clearly. What will be the bride price? What will be the dowry? What will the responsibilities of the bride entail? What must the groom do? What are his obligations as a husband? What are the bride's obligations as a wife? When will the wedding occur? The betrothal is a contract. It is a covenant.

A covenant is an agreement specifying terms and conditions incumbent upon both parties. It is a list of obligations, but it's more than a simple contract. A covenant is the definition of a relationship between two parties. In the ancient culture of the Bible, a covenant's terms and conditions were regarded as being inviolable.

In Exodus 19, God asked Israel to enter into a covenant relationship with him. For his part, he offered to make Israel his "treasured possession, a kingdom of priests, a holy nation." He offered to make them into the people of God. For Israel's part of the deal, her responsibility was to "hear God's voice" and keep the terms of his covenant. His covenant is the Torah. Israel's acceptance of the terms and conditions of the Torah qualified her as the people of God.

Even before hearing the terms and conditions, Israel agreed. The people responded by saying, "All that the LORD has spoken we will do." It is as if God requested Israel's hand in marriage and she consented. She agreed to be his special, intimate people.

No Other Nation

Within the church, we Christians often refer to ourselves as the bride. However, the Torah and all the Scriptures depict Israel as the promised bride. Can there be two brides? Is God a polygamist?

One legend about the giving of the Torah at Mount Sinai says that before God gave the Torah to Israel, he first offered it to all the other nations on earth. Each nation asked to hear the terms involved. Edom could not tolerate a law prohibiting murder. The Ishmaelites could not abide a commandment prohibiting theft. The Ammonites would have nothing to do with a law against immorality. For one reason or another, each nation on earth rejected the Torah. In Exodus 19, however, even before Israel had heard the laws and stipulations of this covenant proposal, they said, "We will do everything the LORD has said." Therefore, the Torah was given to Israel, and through the covenant at Sinai, Israel became the people of God.

To our modern and pluralistic sensibilities, the idea of a singular people of God seems narrow and ethnocentric. Why would God choose one people above all others? Why are the Jewish people the chosen people? Theologians call this seemingly unfair conundrum the "scandal of particularity." Call it what we will, the Bible is clear on this point. Out of all the peoples on the earth, out of all the nations, God has entered into covenant with only one people, only one nation. That nation is Israel. God did not call the Swedes to Mount Sinai. The Irish are not a kingdom of priests. The Italians are not a holy nation. The French are not the people of God. The Americans are not the chosen people.

We should go a step further and point out that God did not call the Baptists to Mount Sinai. The Catholics are not the kingdom of priests. The Lutherans are not the holy nation. The Presbyterians are not the people of God. The Evangelicals are not the chosen people.

God has not made a covenant with any other people on the earth. There is no other nation born by him. If Gentiles want to be a part of the people of God, we have to leave our people and join ourselves to Israel. God has made a covenant with no other nation.

Where then does this leave the Gentiles? Paul says that Gentiles are "excluded from citizenship in Israel and foreigners to the covenants of the promise, without hope and without God in the world." [106] Is this fair? Perhaps not. But God has never played by the rules of men. If he desired to take a single nation for himself, to the exclusion of all other nations, then that is his business. He is, after all, God.

Israel alone, among all the peoples of the earth, enjoys a relationship with the Creator. If the Gentile wants to enter into covenant relationship with the God of Israel, he must enter into the nation of Israel. Another way of saying this is that if the Gentile wants to be saved, he must join the covenant God has made with Israel. How do we enter this covenant? The same way Israel entered the covenant: by agreeing to hear God's voice.

Yeshua invokes the Mount Sinai covenant imagery when he speaks of the Gentile inclusion. In John 10:16 he says, "I have other sheep that are not of this sheep pen. I must bring them also. They too will *hear my voice*, and there shall be one flock and one shepherd" (emphasis added). Notice that there is only one flock, and participation in the flock is based upon listening to the shepherd's voice.

How did Israel become the bride? She did it by agreeing to the terms of his covenant. By agreeing to hear his voice.

God is not a polygamist.

The Voices at Sinai

In the story of the giving of the Torah at Mount Sinai, Exodus 20:18 says, "And all the people saw the thundering."

The Hebrew text of Exodus 20:18 does not actually use the word *thunder*. Instead of thunder, the word *kolot* is employed. *Kolot* is the plural form of the Hebrew *kol*. *Kol* means "voice." So the Torah literally says, "And all the people saw the voices."

The word *kol* (voice) is used as a key word in this passage of Exodus. It is repeated to artfully punctuate the text of Exodus 19 and 20. The children of Israel were brought to Mount Sinai to receive an offer of covenant. Through Moses, the LORD told the children of Israel that if they would indeed "hear his *kol* (voice) and keep his covenant," then they would be his special treasure, his people. "Even though the whole world is mine," he told them, "You will be for me a kingdom of priests and a holy nation."[107] The only contingency was that they must "hear God's voice."

In Hebrew, "hearing someone's voice" is idiomatic for obedience. God was asking Israel for obedience. In order to be his unique and separate people (indeed, to be his bride), Israel had to agree to live in obedience to God's voice. What is his voice? It is the commandments of the Torah, the terms and conditions of his marriage covenant with her.

Three days later, Israel encountered the voices at the mountain. Early in the morning, the cloud descended onto the mountain. There was thunder and lightning and the sound of the trumpet (shofar). Literally translating from Exodus 19:16, we read, "And there were *kolot* (voices) and lightnings, and a heavy cloud upon the mountain, and an exceedingly strong *kol* (voice) of a trumpet; and all the people in the camp trembled."

The revelation of God at Mount Sinai commenced with voices, presumably thunder, accompanied by lightning, and the loud voice of the shofar-trumpet. These voices crescendo into verse 19, which says, "And the *kol* (voice) of the trumpet was growing, and exceedingly strong! And Moses spoke, and God answered him in a *kol* (voice)."

All the people heard the voice of God as he spoke the Ten Commandments. It was an unprecedented and not-to-be-repeated moment in the history of the universe. An entire nation literally heard the voice of God speaking. They did not hear God in an ethereal or quasi-spiritual sense. Rather, they audibly heard the voice of God speaking—a vivid dramatization of the idiom employed at the beginning of the story: "If you will indeed hear my *kol* (voice)."

Seventy Voices

By the time we come to Exodus 20:18, "And all the people saw the voices," (author's translation) we have already learned that the voices are the voice of God.

Most translations smooth out the Hebrew of Exodus 20:18 by translating the word *voices* as "thunder." Thunder agrees with the context of the thunder and lightning at Mount Sinai. The sages of the midrash, however, read the passage literally, without our glosses. Based on their literal reading of the Hebrew, they derived a legend about the voices of God at Mount Sinai. In the *Midrash Rabbah*, Rabbi Yochanan wondered about the implications of God revealing himself in a multitude of voices.

> The Torah says, "And all the people saw the voices." Note that it does not say "the voice," but "the voices"; wherefore Rabbi Yochanan said that God's voice, as it was uttered, split up into seventy voices, in seventy languages, so that all the nations should understand. (*Shemot Rabbah* 5:9)

The Talmud also quotes Rabbi Yochanan's tradition of the seventy voices at Mount Sinai. In the Talmudic version, Rabbi Yochanan is explaining a verse from Psalm 68. The verse reads, "The LORD announced the Word, and great was the company of those who proclaimed it."[108] Rabbi Yochanan explained the great company of proclaimers to be the multifaceted voice of God that speaks in the seventy languages:

> Rabbi Yochanan said: "What is meant by the verse, 'The Lord announced the word, and great was the company of those who proclaimed it'? Every single word that went forth from [God] was split up into seventy languages."
> (b.*Shabbat* 88b)

What did Rabbi Yochanan mean? In the world of rabbinic thought and literature, all of humanity is divided into seventy families of mankind. The number is derived from the seventy descendants of Noah's sons in Genesis 10. Talmudic literature frequently speaks of the "seventy nations," meaning all nations. The seventy nations are to be understood as idiomatic for all mankind. At Babel, each family of man was given a language. When the sages speak of the seventy languages, it is to be understood as all languages.

Rabbi Yochanan is telling us that as God spoke the words of Torah at Mount Sinai, his voice spoke simultaneously in all the languages of the world. Why? So that all mankind might hear and receive the Torah in their own language. The Torah is meant to have universal appeal. It is an open invitation to all mankind. The Torah is offered to anyone who will "hear God's voice and keep his covenant." Anyone can be part of the marriage. Anyone can join the bride.

Another legend has it that the Torah was given in the wilderness, which belonged to no particular nation, so that all nations could have access to it. There is a deep universalism implied here that seems to contradict the particularity of Israel's divine selection. Only Israel was able to enter into covenant with God and become the people of God. Israel alone is a kingdom of priests and God's holy people. However, the invitation to Israel's covenant is left wide open to all mankind.

The legend of the Torah in seventy languages appears again at Mount Ebal. In Deuteronomy 27, Moses commanded Israel to erect an altar on Mount Ebal. They were to build an altar as part of a covenant renewal ceremony. They were to plaster over the stones of the altar and write all the words of the Torah "very clearly" upon the altar.[109] In Joshua 8, the children of Israel arrived at Shechem and built the altar on Mount Ebal as Moses commanded them.

The Mishnah records the details of the ceremony. In the Mishnah, we read that the Israelites wrote out the whole Torah in seventy languages on the altar. "They brought the stones and built the altar and plastered it with lime. Then they wrote on it all the words of the Torah in seventy tongues, as it is written, 'very clearly.'"[110]

When the Hebrew Scriptures were translated into Greek, the Greek Bible was called the "Seventy" (Septuagint, LXX). Again, the image is of the Torah going forth in all tongues. How are we to understand this idea?

When God offered the Torah to Israel, he offered it as the terms by which Israel could become his bride, his special treasure. However, the offer made to Israel does not exclude non-Israelites. Anyone from any nation who will hear God's voice and keep his covenant will be included in this relationship. Anyone who responds to God's invitation to covenant relationship is welcome to join the peculiar people and take a place among the kingdom of priests.

Paul reasoned it out in the book of Romans by asking us, "Is God the God of Jews only? Is he not the God of Gentiles too?"[111] Clearly, he is the God of the Gentiles too. His Torah is an open invitation to the whole world.

The Voice of Fire

In Exodus 19 and 20, God stepped down onto Mount Sinai. He spoke the Ten Commandments in the hearing of all the people. At the end of the narrative we read, "And all the people saw the voices and the torches."

We would normally smooth out the Hebrew of verse 18 by translating the word saw as "heard" and by translating the word torches as "lightning." Thus we can paraphrase, "And all the people heard the thunder and saw the lightning." The sages, however, read the passage literally, without our glosses. Based upon their literal reading of the Hebrew, the people saw voices and torches.

What does it mean, "the people saw voices"? How does one see a sound? How does one see a voice? Where did the torches come from?

In Deuteronomy, Moses retold the story of hearing God's voice at Sinai. In ten different passages, he reminded Israel that they heard God's voice speak to them "from out of the fire." Repeatedly he said, "You all heard the voice speaking from out of the fire."

Regarding this fiery voice of God, the disciples of Rabbi Ishmael applied a verse from Jeremiah. The verse says, "'Is not my word like fire,' declares the LORD, 'and like a hammer that breaks a rock in pieces?'"[112] Rabbi Ishmael imagined God's voice at Mount Sinai to be like a sledgehammer breaking up large stones. With each successive blow a multitude of fiery sparks are scattered in every direction.

> The School of R. Ishmael taught the meaning of the verse: "And like a hammer that breaks a rock in pieces." Just as a hammer is divided into many sparks, so too every single word that went forth from the Holy One, blessed be He, split up into seventy languages. (b.*Shabbat* 88b)

According to that interpretation, the voice of God at Mount Sinai not only split into seventy voices speaking seventy different tongues, but those voices were like hot sparks flying forth from a hammer's blows on stone. All the people really did see the voice of God, and torches too, because the voice of God appeared to them like hot, burning torches. As God spoke, his words took shape as torches of fire:

> On the occasion of [the giving of] the Torah, the [children of Israel] not only heard the LORD's Voice, but actually saw the sound waves as they emerged from the LORD's mouth. They visualized them as a fiery substance. Each commandment that left the LORD's mouth traveled around the entire camp and then came back to every Jew individually. (*Midrash Chazit*)[113]

At Mount Sinai, the LORD told Israel, "If you will hear my voice … you will be for me a kingdom of priests and a holy nation." Israel not only heard the voice of God at Mount Sinai, they heard it in every language. They saw it too. His voice came to them as fire.

The Voice of Pentecost

Another ancient Jewish tradition about the giving of the Torah at Mount Sinai has to do with the timing of the event. Judaism regards the festival of Shavuot (Pentecost) to be the anniversary of the day on which God spoke at Sinai. The festival is celebrated as the festival of the giving of the Torah. In the synagogue, a wedding contract between God and Israel is read on Shavuot. The whole congregation recites the Ten Commandments together on Shavuot. Exodus chapters 19 and 20 are publicly read on Shavuot. Pentecost (Shavuot) is the day the giving of the Torah is remembered and re-enacted. It is celebrated as a wedding anniversary for God and his bride. Therefore, the Feast of Shavuot, in Jewish tradition, is also the anniversary of the day when God's voice spoke in all languages of the world and was visible as torches of fire that came "to every Jew individually."

In Acts 2, Shimon Peter and the other disciples were gathered to celebrate this wedding anniversary—the festival of Shavuot—when the Holy Spirit fell upon them in the form of tongues of fire. Torches of fire came to rest on each individual disciple. As a literary device and as a genuine supernatural phenomenon, the miracle is an allusion to the legend of God's fiery voice at Mount Sinai. In addition, subsequent to receiving this fiery spirit, the disciples found themselves proclaiming the gospel in every language. The miracle of speaking in all tongues is another allusion to the giving of the Torah at Mount Sinai. It is a literal fulfillment of the psalm later quoted by Rabbi Yochanan: "The LORD announced the word, and great was the company of those who proclaimed it."[114]

Whether or not the tradition of the seventy languages at Sinai and the fiery words at Sinai preserve actual historical memories of the Mount Sinai experience is not of great consequence. It is consequential, however, to remember that Peter and the disciples and followers of Yeshua were all well aware of the Pentecost legends. We can only assume that those legends predate the book of Acts; otherwise, the allusions would be lost. They must have known the story of the giving of the Torah, the words of fire resting on each individual, and the voice of God speaking to all mankind in every language on Pentecost. The miracles, signs, and wonders that came upon them in Acts 2 carried deep significance. The tongues of fire and the speaking in every tongue were both direct allusions to the Mount Sinai wedding experience and the receiving of the Torah. God was underscoring the inseparable relationship between his Holy Spirit and his holy Torah.

A Voice to the Jewish People

As Shimon Peter and the other believers who were gathered on that fateful Pentecost began to preach the gospel, their words were uttered in every language. Jewish people from all over the world were present in Jerusalem to celebrate the feast of Pentecost. Luke lists fifteen place names and nations from which they had come. Each person heard the gospel being proclaimed in his own native tongue.

Luke is careful to point out that those assembled there that day were all Jewish. He prefaces his description of the event by saying, "And there were dwelling at Jerusalem Jews, devout men, out of every nation under heaven."[115] They were devout Jews from a variety of locales. They represented the wide diversity of the first-century Diaspora. But they were all Jews, or at the very least, proselytes to Judaism. Even the "strangers from Rome" in Acts 2:10 are described as "both Jews and proselytes."

As Peter spoke to the crowd, he addressed them as "all Israel." The term "all Israel" is a common way of speaking of Diaspora Judaism even today. Peter's address was meant in that regard. His message is not just for those assembled, but for all Jewish people everywhere.

Undoubtedly there were also Gentiles present, God-fearers and the like, but they were not part of the story, nor were they included in Peter's address to "all Israel." In Acts 2, Peter had not yet even considered the possibility of Gentile participation outside of a legal conversion to Judaism.

Luke goes to some pains to make sure we understand that the faith was Jewish up through this point in his narrative. It is important for Luke to show us that the gospel is received only by Jews, because he is setting us up for the central conflict of the book of Acts (indeed, the dramatic theme of the whole book): the controversy over the Gentile inclusion in the kingdom. It is a controversy that does not erupt until Acts 10 and the conversion of Cornelius.

In subsequent chapters of Acts we meet the Ethiopian eunuch, but there is no reason to assume he was not Jewish. Ethiopian Jews are with us to this day. We also see Samaritan conversions, but even Samaritans are quasi-Israelites. They are not quite Gentiles. Not until Acts 10 are Gentile believers formally introduced into the mix.

A Voice to the Nations

After Shimon Peter took the gospel to Cornelius, the Gentile, and his household, he returned to a less than enthusiastic welcome among the Jewish believers in Jerusalem. "The apostles and the brothers throughout Judea heard that the Gentiles also had received the word of God. So when Peter went up to Jerusalem, the circumcised believers criticized him."[116] Shimon Peter found himself in a defensive posture, explaining his radical decisions. It must have seemed radical even to him.

When he had arrived at Cornelius's house, he had said, "I now realize how true it is that God does not show favoritism but accepts men from every nation who fear him and do what is right."[117] That kind of thinking was a dramatic reversal of Peter's theology. Prior to his vision of the sheet and the unclean animals,[118] Peter assumed that God certainly did show favoritism. After all, wasn't the nation of Israel God's special treasure, his kingdom of priests and his holy nation? Prior to his vision, Peter must have assumed that the gospel of Yeshua was meant only for Israel. He even intimates as much when he refers to the gospel as the "message God sent to the people of Israel."[119]

Cornelius and his household were not Jews. They certainly were not Israelites. They were pureblooded Gentiles without a claim or status in Israel. Hence Peter referred to Cornelius as "one of another nation."[120] The people gathered in Cornelius's house were not the people of Israel. They were strangers to the covenant.

Imagine Peter's surprise. Imagine the surprise of the other Jews who had come with him. We read, "The circumcised believers who had come with Peter were astonished that the gift of the Holy Spirit had been poured out even on the Gentiles. For they heard them speaking in tongues."[121]

The significance of the miracle could not have been lost on Peter. It was God's confirmation that the gospel was also meant for the Gentiles. Just as the voice of God was split into the seventy languages of the Gentiles at Mount Sinai (according to the legends), just as the Jewish believers had spoken the gospel in all the languages of the nations at Shavuot, now the Gentiles in Cornelius's house were experiencing the same miracle. The voice of God was speaking in various languages to them and through them. They had not gone through a legal conversion ritual. They were still Gentiles.

When Peter heard them speaking in the "seventy languages," he could no longer theologically exclude those Gentiles from Israel. They had heard the voice of God, just as Israel had heard it at Mount Sinai. They had heard the voice of God, and the promise was that anyone who heard his voice would be God's special treasure, a kingdom of priests and a holy people: Israel. That was the promise of the betrothal.

Confident in the definitive sign of the seventy languages, Peter cried out, "Can anyone keep these people from being baptized with water? They have received the Holy Spirit just as we have."[122]

The First Epistle of Peter

For Gentiles making a legal conversion into Judaism according to the traditionally prescribed ritual, immersion is supposed to follow circumcision. Circumcision is the sign of entering the covenant. Immersion is a symbolic death and rebirth. The Gentile going down into the water of immersion is said to die to his old Gentile self. As he emerged from the water, he is said to be "reborn" as a Jew. The term "born again" originally referred to this symbolic rebirth as a Jew.[123] In Judaism, one who has undergone a ritual conversion of circumcision and baptism is no longer referred to as a Gentile. He has been born again. He is a Jew and a full-blooded part of Israel.

In the case of Cornelius and his household, Peter took the almost unprecedented step of forgoing circumcision. I say "almost unprecedented" because there is a minority opinion in the Talmud that states one who is immersed, though not circumcised, is still regarded as an Israelite. Rabbi Yehoshua reasoned that if immersion was sufficient to mark a woman's conversion, it was sufficient for a man as well:

> "If a man went through the prescribed immersion but had not been circumcised," Rabbi Yehoshua said, "behold he is a proper proselyte; for so we find that the mothers [Sarah, Rivkah, Rachel, and Leah] went through ritual immersion but had not been circumcised." (b. *Yevamot* 46a)

For Peter, the evidence of the miraculous voices in every language was compelling enough. He needed no further convincing of the covenantal status of the Gentile believers.

The change in Peter's theology is evidenced in his first epistle. The epistle of 1 Peter is a book written to Gentile believers. Internal evidence suggests that it may have been written for new converts on the day of their baptism.

That the Gentile believers are the subjects of 1 Peter is clear from the outset. Peter contrasts their current state with "the evil desires you had when you lived in ignorance."[124] He reminds them, "You were redeemed from the empty way of life handed down to you from your forefathers." Peter also reminds his readers that in the past, they did "what Gentiles choose to do—living in debauchery, lust, drunkenness, orgies, carousing and detestable idolatry."[125] However, since their conversion, he no longer regards them as Gentiles. Instead, they are "God's Chosen, strangers in the world,"[126] the "born again."[127] They are like "new born babies."[128]

Peter points out to his readers that they are not included in God's household on the basis of their own bloodlines. They are not the natural seed of Abraham. Rather, they are part of the people of God on the basis of "an imperishable seed" planted in them "through the living and enduring word of God."[129] This means that the seed implanted in them is not implanted by means of sexual reproduction. Rather, the seed implanted in them is by means of the power of the word of God.

As a result, they are no longer Gentiles. Instead, they are to live exemplary lives "among the Gentiles,"[130] but they themselves "are a chosen people, a royal priesthood, a holy nation, a people belonging to God."[131]

"Chosen people," "royal priesthood," "holy nation," and "people belonging to God" are all titles of Israel. They are the very roles God offered to Israel at Mount Sinai if only she would "hear his voice and keep his covenant." Now the Gentiles have heard the voice that offered the Torah in the seventy languages of the nations. They have entered that covenant, to keep it through the auspices of Yeshua. They have become a part of Israel the bride.

As Gentile believers, we find our position in Israel spelled out here. We are no longer to be regarded as merely Gentiles. We are part of the people of God. We have become a "chosen people, a royal priesthood, a holy nation, a people belonging to God." We have been so made on the basis of an "imperishable seed" planted in us "through the living and enduring word of God," not a perishable seed inherited from distant ancestors, nor on the basis of a legal conversion. We have become a part of the people of Israel.

The People of God

1 Peter 2:10 says, "Once you were not a people, but now you are the people of God; once you had not received mercy, but now you have received mercy." Peter borrowed these words from the prophet Hosea.

Hosea used a similar phrase to give hope to Israel in a time of apostasy. In the book of Hosea, the ten northern tribes had failed to keep God's covenant and had forgotten to hear his voice. Their disobedience had resulted in alienation from God. The LORD told them, "You are not my people, and I am not your God." He compared them to an unfaithful wife. The bride of God was to be divorced.

He did not leave them hopeless and dejected. Rather, he told them of a day of repentance, a day when they would return to him. He said, "Yet the Israelites will be like the sand on the seashore, which cannot be measured or counted. In the place where it was said to them, 'You are not my people,' they will be called 'sons of the living God.'"[132] It is a prophecy of the ultimate reign of Messiah in the Kingdom to come.

Peter seized upon the image because it was deftly applicable to the Gentile converts to whom he was writing. The Gentiles, like Israel in the day of her apostasy, were previously alienated from God. They were not God's people. They did not know God's mercy. Now, like Israel in the future day of her repentance, the Gentiles had become "sons of the living God." Peter declared to his Gentile converts, "Once you were not a people, but now you are the people of God; once you had not received mercy, but now you have received mercy."[133] Paul uses the same passage for the same purpose in Romans 9.

As Peter wrote to his former Gentiles, he was transmitting the voice of God from Mount Sinai as it was split into the seventy languages of the nations. He was carrying out the commandment of his Master: "Therefore go and make disciples of all nations, baptizing them in the name of the Father and of the Son and of the Holy Spirit, and teaching them to obey everything I have commanded you."

9
DAVID'S FALLEN SUKKAH

Acts 15

Jerusalem in the year 49 CE.

The council of the elders has been convened. Seventy bearded Jews have crowded into the hall and seated themselves in a half circle. Two more Jewish men are standing in front of them giving testimony. The elders are listening intently.

This is not the Sanhedrin, but like the Sanhedrin, these seventy men are legislators. Like the Sanhedrin, their word is the final authority. They are the highest court of appeal among the believers. The decisions these men implement are binding on all the congregations of believers.

Among these elders are several familiar faces. Most of them were among the seventy disciples of Yeshua. Some of them were even numbered among the Twelve. Isn't this one who is seated up close John the son of Zebedee? And the fellow with the parchments is certainly Matthew the tax collector. Shimon Peter is present.

The president of the council is none other than Yaakov HaTzaddik: James the Righteous, the son of Joseph. He is James the brother of Yeshua, and he even bears some resemblance to him. He is young to be at the head of such a venerable assembly, but over the years he has won the confidence of his brother's disciples. The congregations of believers throughout the world look to the men of the Jerusalem Council for leadership and guidance, and the council, in turn, looks to James for the same.

The two men giving testimony are Paul and Barnabas. They have come from Antioch. They are reporting the results of their work among the Gentiles. Paul cannot contain his zeal as he retells their adventures. His hands are waving and his beard is wagging as he talks. Everywhere they went, everywhere they preached, God opened the door of faith to the Gentiles. The Gentiles in every city turned to Yeshua. His obvious enthusiasm is contagious, and smiles are spreading among the elders.

Then there is an interruption.

The Pharisees Object

Just as the testimony of Paul and Barnabas is beginning, several of the elders stand to their feet, a dozen or more men. Like Paul, these men are Pharisees. But they are also zealous believers in Messiah and brothers in the kingdom. They wait for James to give them permission to speak.

James acknowledges them and gives them the floor. Paul and Barnabas sit down.

The spokesman for the believing Pharisees steps forward and addresses the council.

"Brothers," he charges, "the Gentile believers must be circumcised and required to obey the Torah of Moses."[134]

He means that if a Gentile desires salvation and participation in the kingdom, he must make a full and formal conversion to Judaism. According to this opinion, nothing less than a full conversion to Judaism will be adequate to ensure salvation. The charge has been made, and the brother Pharisees return to their seats.

The elders debate the issue for hours. The arguments are heated and loud. Proof texts are cited to support one side, and then more proofs are presented to support the other. "Have you not read?" "Is it not written?" "Have you never seen where it says?" Each opinion is backed with Scripture and full conviction. Each of the elders is convinced of the unassailable veracity of his own particular argument.

They aren't arguing about whether Gentiles are allowed to keep Torah. That is not the question set before them. The question they are arguing is whether Gentiles must be circumcised and come under the full obligation of Torah in order to merit salvation. There is a world of difference between those two questions. Circumcision stands for a legal and formal conversion to Judaism. The question is, "Must Gentiles legally convert to Judaism—becoming Jewish—in order to be saved?"

The objection of Paul's opponents is based upon the "theology of particularity" that characterizes Judaism. Israel alone is the chosen people. Israel alone is God's inheritance and special treasure. There is ample Scripture to support such a notion. To even consider opening the door of particularity to any and every ethnicity is to compromise that select status. Uncircumcised Philistines in the kingdom of heaven, sitting at the table with Abraham, Isaac, and Jacob? Unthinkable! Borderline blasphemy!

SHIMON'S REBUTTAL

At long last, all the voices have been heard. Everyone has had a chance to say his piece, except for one lone elder: Shimon, who is called Peter. Shimon Peter stands and takes the floor. "Brothers, you know that some time ago God made a choice among you that the Gentiles might hear from my lips the message of the Gospel and believe."[135]

Everyone remembers the incident in Caesarea. Everyone remembers the debate that was sparked those many years ago when Peter returned with word of the conversion of a Roman centurion and his whole family.

Peter continues, "God, who knows the heart, showed that he accepted those Gentiles by giving the Holy Spirit to them, just as he did to us. He made no distinction between them and us, for he purified their hearts by faith. Now then, why do you try to test God by putting on the necks of the disciples a yoke that neither we nor our fathers have been able to bear? No! We believe it is through the grace of our Lord Yeshua that we are saved, just as they are."[136]

Peter's argument is simple. He points out that even Jews are not saved through their obedience to the Torah. If used as a means to attain salvation, the Torah would be an unbearable yoke. Generation after generation of Jewish history has proven that all men sin and fall short of the glory of God. No one is saved through keeping the Torah. Instead, salvation for the Jewish believers comes through the grace of Yeshua. "Why would it be any different for Gentiles?" Peter asks.

He sits back down. His argument leaves the men quietly thinking. No one can offer a rebuttal. Heads are nodding.

JAMES'S PROPOSAL

James returns the floor to Paul and Barnabas. They continue with their testimony. They tell the stories of the places they have been and the people they have met. There was the adventure with the sorcerer in Paphos. The crippled man in Lystra. The priests of Zeus who tried to sacrifice to them. There was Pisidian Antioch, Iconium, Attalia, and of course Antioch itself. God's spirit had worked amazing wonders in every city they visited. There were miracles and more to tell about. Everywhere they went, Gentiles were receiving the gospel, and they were receiving it by faith.

With their stories finally told, James takes the floor. All eyes are upon him. He is going to introduce an opinion that the council will have to vote to approve or disapprove. "Brothers, listen to me," he begins warmly and with a broad, sweeping gesture. "Shimon has described to us how God at first showed his concern by taking from the Gentiles a people for himself. The words of the prophets are in agreement with this, as it is written: 'After this I will return and rebuild David's fallen tent. Its ruins I will rebuild, and I will restore it, that the remnant of men may seek the LORD, and all the Gentiles who bear my Name, says the LORD, who does these things that have been known for ages.' It is my judgment, therefore, that we should not make it difficult for the Gentiles who are turning to God."[137]

"What does he mean by "we should not make it diffcult for the Gentiles"? The meaning is clear enough. We should not require conversion (circumcision) and observance of the entire Torah from them."

How is this possible? Is nothing required of the Gentile believers then? Are they just to add faith in Yeshua to their paganism and carry on as if they had never heard the gospel?

No, of course not. James continues to explain, "Instead we should write to the Gentile believers, telling them to abstain from food polluted by idols, from sexual immorality, from the meat of strangled animals, and from blood. For Moses has been preached in every city from the earliest times and is read in the synagogues on every Sabbath."[138]

THE FOUR ESSENTIALS

James introduces four minimum laws for Gentile believers. Conspicuously absent are some major commandments, such as honoring one's father and mother and the prohibition against murder. The four laws James selects are socially obvious ones that will enable the Gentile converts to move among Jews. They are to abstain from meat sacrificed to idols, from meats that are not slaughtered in a kosher manner, from the consumption of blood, and from sexual immorality. These four laws are not presented as if they are a replacement for the Torah, nor are they meant as the four minimum commandments that will merit salvation. They seem to be intended as a basic set of rules that will enable Jews and Gentiles to congregate together. The food laws prohibiting blood, un-slaughtered meat, and meat contaminated by idols provide a minimum table standard. The four laws also target specific facets of Hellenistic paganism: blood rituals, idolatry, ritual feasts, and sexual immorality (whether overt temple prostitution or covert promiscuity). Each of these prohibitions applies specifically to the social and religious conflicts that separates Jews and Gentiles from one another. The four laws ensured that the Gentiles would be able to enjoy fellowship within the Jewish synagogue communities.

According to James's proposal, it would not be necessary for a new Gentile believer to understand and fulfill all the complex laws and traditional prohibitions of Sabbath before being reckoned part of a congregation of believers. But such a Gentile would need to make certain immediate changes in order to be received by that same congregation. Under James's proposal, the Gentile believer would not need to have his foreskin removed in order to be considered a brother in Messiah. However, he would have to give up consorting with Diana's temple prostitutes before the hand of fellowship would be extended to him.

The Rest of the Torah

As for the rest of the laws of the written Torah, James neither binds their observance upon the Gentile believers, nor does he completely exempt the believers from them. Instead he says, "Moses has been preached in every city from the earliest times and is read in the synagogues on every Sabbath."[139]

Christian commentators usually suggest that James' statement about Moses being read and preached in the synagogue every week is meant only to assuage the Pharisees present. "After all," says James with a wink at the Pharisees, "Moses is taught in the synagogue every week. Therefore, Torah doesn't have any real bearing on the Gentile believers." But that's absurd. James's could hardly pacify the Pharisaic party at the same time he dismissed their very argument. Instead, his words seem to buttress their contention: "Torah is being taught in every city. There is no excuse not to learn it and do it."

One Messianic Jewish interpretation suggests that James was merely pointing out how ineffective the teaching of the Torah had been in the past. In other words, he was saying, "The Torah has always been taught. It's never brought Gentiles to faith before, so let's forget about Torah for Gentiles." This explanation hardly makes sense either. On the contrary, first-century Diaspora Judaism was very attractive to Gentiles and had drawn significant numbers into the folds of Judaism.

So what did James mean?

His words mean exactly what they say. The Torah is read in the synagogue every week. At this early time in the development of the Messianic faith, the believers were still assembling within the synagogues and meeting in homes. Not until Paul moves his house of study out of the Corinth synagogue and into the next-door house of Titius Justus do we see a clear change of venue where believers assemble outside of the local synagogue—and that doesn't happen until Acts 18. At the time of the Jerusalem Council, Jewish and Gentile believers were still assembling in the local synagogue every Shabbat.[140] And in those synagogues, the Torah was read every week.

So regarding the question of Gentile believers and their obligations toward the Torah, James says, "The Torah is read and preached in the assembly every week." That is to say that the Gentile believers will hear the Torah. They will hear it every week. They will hear it preached every week. The obvious expectation is that hearing it read and hearing it preached should eventually lead to doing it. Given time to hear and study, the Gentile believers might eventually learn the ways of observance. Yet this was not to be a requirement placed upon them.

One might paraphrase James' words as "Let's not make things difficult for these new believers. Have them do a couple of basic things so they don't get tossed out of the fellowship, but as for the rest of the Torah, they will be hearing it every week."

Are Gentile believers required to keep the Torah to earn salvation? No.

Are Gentile believers required to keep Torah at all? Of course. Unfortunately, the apostles never spelled out the details of their expectation. James and the council did not say whether they envisioned Gentiles becoming fully Torah observant or not. They left the matter of the Gentile's relationship to Torah and Judaism ambiguous and unresolved. But they did not close the door.

As a proof text for the legitimacy of his proposal, James cites a passage from Amos.

The Proof Text

The Amos passage is important to consider. What does that particular prophecy mean, and why did James believe it justifies the decision to allow Gentiles into the kingdom of heaven? Studying the passage is complicated by the fact that Acts quotes the Septuagint version of the passage. There is a significant variation between the Greek LXX (Septuagint) reading and the Hebrew reading of Amos 9:12. We had best consider both versions of the text.

The New International Version translates the Hebrew of Amos 9:11–12 as follows:

> In that day I will restore David's fallen tent. I will repair its broken places, restore its ruins, and build it as it used to be, so that they may possess the remnant of Edom and all the nations that bear my Name," declares the LORD, who will do these things. (Amos 9:11–12)

The word the NIV translates as "tent" is the Hebrew word *sukkah*, which means "booth or hut." Look at the condition of David's *sukkah*. It is toppled. It has broken places and ruins. It is not what it used to be, but one day it will be set back up and repaired. David's fallen *sukkah* is the dynastic rule of the house of David. It is the Davidic monarchy.

Even in the days of Amos, the Davidic monarchy wasn't what it had been. David's house used to rule over a united Israel. All twelve tribes served under David and under David's son Solomon. There was peace and prosperity when all the tribes of Israel were unified under the shelter of David's *sukkah*. But Amos lived in a time when ten of the twelve tribes were outside of the Davidic monarchy. They had their own king, Jeroboam II. They had their own capital and their own holy places. The Davidic monarchy, which used to rule over all the tribes of Israel, retained only two tribes: Judah and Benjamin. By comparison to what it once was, it had collapsed.

The prophet saw that one day David's house would collapse completely and there would be no king from the line of David sitting on the throne of Israel or Judah. But after that, Amos tells us, David's fallen *sukkah* will be rebuilt. The dynasty will be restored. A new Davidic king will sit on the throne of all Israel again. The broken places of the monarchy will be repaired; the ruins of David's dynasty will be restored.

When that happens, the house of David will possess the "remnant of Edom and all the nations that bear [the LORD's] Name." It is a picture of the prophetic ideal. Things will return to the way they were in the good old days. It will be like it was in the days of Solomon, when Edom was a vassal state of Israel and all the nations brought tribute to King Solomon in Jerusalem. A Davidic king will rule out of Jerusalem. His house will possess Edom and all the nations will be subject to him, and all the nations subject to him will bear the LORD's Name.

The Gentile nations who bear God's Name are nations like those the prophet invokes in Amos 9:7: "Are not you Israelites the same to me as the *Cushites*? Did I not bring Israel up from *Egypt*, the *Philistines* from *Caphtor*, and the *Arameans* from *Kir*?" (emphasis added). God's point is that he is working with other nations too. He is not just the God of Israel; he is the God of the whole world. His plan of redemption is universal in scope and not limited only to Israel. When David's fallen *sukkah* is restored, all these nations that he has patiently worked with will bear God's Name and become the possession of the house of David. They will be ruled by the king of Israel as part of the commonwealth of Israel.

The Septuagint reading of Amos 9:12 is slightly different. According to the book of Acts, James quotes a reading of the Hebrew closer to the Septuagint's rendering of the passage. That version of the passage tells us that David's fallen *sukkah* will be restored so "that the remnant of men, and all the Gentiles upon whom my Name is called, may earnestly seek me."[141] Therefore, the purpose of a restored Davidic king is that all mankind may seek God.

This Septuagint version apparently read the Hebrew *Edom* as *adam*, meaning all mankind. The two variants are not contradictory; rather, they complement each other's meanings. According to the traditional Hebrew reading, the restored Davidic dynasty will possess the remnant of Edom (a Gentile nation) and, in fact, all the nations that bear God's Name. According to the LXX reading, the Davidic dynasty will be restored so that the aforementioned nations may seek the LORD.

In either case, the Gentiles who bear God's Name are Gentile nations who will be subject to an Israelite monarchy, a monarchy that will afford them the opportunity to seek the LORD.

The Proof Is in the Prophets

How does this passage legitimize the decision of James and the Jerusalem Council? In what way does this passage justify a Gentile exemption from circumcision, conversion to Judaism, and full liability to the laws of the Torah?

The key to understanding how James uses the passage is in identifying the Davidic King. To James and the believers in Jerusalem, David's restored *sukkah* is Yeshua.[142] He is the Davidic king who has come to rebuild the monarchy of Israel. Yeshua is the repairer of the broken places, the restorer of the ruins, who rebuilds the legitimate throne of Israel. According to the Amos passage, the restored Davidic kingdom will include those Gentiles who bear God's Name.

The Gentiles whom Paul and Barnabas were encountering fit the prophet's description. They were Gentiles from the nations who identified themselves with God's Name and sought after God because of the kingship of Yeshua. However, if all Gentiles who seek the LORD through Yeshua must convert to Judaism and legally become Jews, they cease to be reckoned as Gentiles at all. By virtue of the fact that Amos calls them Gentiles who bear God's Name and seek the LORD, they cannot be Jews or even proselytes. The moment that they were legally converted to Judaism, they would become Jews and no longer be Gentiles who bear God's Name and seek the LORD. They would fail to fulfill the prophecy because the prophecy clearly speaks of these God-seekers as Gentiles. For the prophecy to be literally fulfilled, both Jews and Gentiles must exist in the days of Messiah—an impossibility if all Gentiles were forced to become legally Jewish.

Amos's Gentiles are to be vassals of the Jewish king. As such, they are to be part of the commonwealth of Israel, with rights as citizens of Israel. They are to be bound to the laws of the king of Israel. By blood, they are Edomites, Cushites, Philistines, Arameans, and peoples of every tribe, tongue, and nation on earth. They are to be regarded as Gentiles, bearing God's Name, seeking the LORD, and serving the restored Davidic dynasty, even Yeshua the King. They have a legitimate place in the kingdom, but they still maintain their own ethnic identity.

10
GENTILE ISRAEL

Galatians

Apparently, not everyone agreed with the decision of the Jerusalem council.

Consider, for example, the situation in Galatia. The Galatians were new believers, converts out of paganism. They were the Gentiles of the cities of Pisidian Antioch, Iconium, and Derbe. Faith in Yeshua was their only rite of conversion. But subsequent to their conversion out of the kingdom of darkness and into the kingdom of God, some brothers and sisters, perhaps from Jerusalem, paid them a visit. These visitors held fast to the conviction that only ethnic and legal Jews could have a place in God's covenant. Only Israel could be saved. Only Israel was in the kingdom.

The visitors taught that it was necessary, in addition to faith in Yeshua, for the Galatian Gentiles to be circumcised—thereby signifying their formal and legal conversion to Judaism. According to these fellows, only after circumcision could the Gentiles be regarded as truly a part of the kingdom. Faith in Messiah alone was not adequate.

Paul responded to this teaching with his scathing letter to the Galatians. He lost his temper and accused them of teaching some other gospel. He said, "Let them be eternally condemned!"[143] He even took it a step further than that. He said, "As for those agitators, I wish they would go the whole way and emasculate themselves!"[144] Consider what the apostle is saying: As if eternal damnation was not bad enough, Paul wanted them to be eternally damned with less than their whole apparatus.

Paul's rancor reveals his priorities. The gospel of salvation, full and free, specifically salvation proclaimed to the Gentiles, salvation by faith through grace, was the very heartbeat of passion that fueled the old Pharisee's life. The Gentile inclusion through faith in Yeshua was the gospel to Paul. That was the good news. To him, anything that obscured that simple truth was some other gospel.

THE APOSTLE TO THE UNCIRCUMCISED

Subsequent to the Jerusalem Council of Acts 15, Paul referred to himself as the official "apostle to the Gentiles," as in Romans 11:13, for example. The Greek word he uses for Gentiles is *ethnos*, from which we derive the word "ethnicity." Paul identified himself as the apostle to the ethnic nationalities. His description of his apostleship is contrasted against Peter's apostleship to the Jews.

> They saw that I had been entrusted with the task of preaching the gospel to the uncircumcised, just as Peter had been to the circumcised. For God, who was at work in the ministry of Peter as an apostle to the circumcised, was also at work in my ministry as an apostle to the Gentiles. (Galatians 2:7–8)

In this passage, Paul uses the term uncircumcised (*akrobustia*) synonymously with the term Gentiles (*ethnos*). From Paul's perspective, to be uncircumcised was to be a Gentile, one from the nations. The Greek word *akrobustia*, which we are translating as "uncircumcised," is perhaps more honestly rendered as "foreskinned." It is a contraction of two Greek words. *Akron* means tip or extremity. *Posthe* means the masculine member. The *akrobustia* is the extremity of that masculine member's tip; that is, the foreskin. The gentlemen Paul referred to as *akrobustia* would have been men still in possession of such.

Peter, on the other hand, is the apostle to the *peritome*; that is, the circumcised.

But wait! Suppose you didn't have a foreskin. Take Paul's convert Lydia, for example: a weaver of purple cloth and, more to the point, a woman. Was she outside of Paul's purview because she was a woman and he was the apostle to the foreskinned? The point that needs to be understood is that the term "foreskinned" does not necessarily refer to the literal state of being circumcised or uncircumcised. It is used categorically to refer to those Gentile believers who had not made a conversion to Judaism. In a similar way, the term "circumcision" is used categorically to refer to Jews and to proselytes who have become Jewish through a legal conversion ritual. That's why Paul is able to say, "Circumcision is nothing and uncircumcision is nothing. Keeping God's commands is what counts."[145] Notice the apparent contradiction: Circumcision is one of God's commands. If keeping God's commands is what counts, then surely circumcision is something. The way Paul uses the term, circumcision refers specifically to the legal conversion ritual. Thus Paul is saying, "As regards one's standing before God, legal conversion to Judaism is meaningless. Keeping God's commands is what counts."

Paul, then, is the apostle to the "foreskinned," by which he means Gentiles. Peter is the apostle to the "circumcised," by which Paul means Jews and proselytes to Judaism. If a foreskinned person (*akrobustia*) should choose to undergo a legal conversion ritual, which includes circumcision (*peritome*), he would be no longer regarded as a Gentile (*ethnos*). Indeed, such a person becomes legally Jewish.

Paul, the apostle to the foreskinned, was zealous to defend the Gentiles' right to retain their foreskins. If they were compelled to be circumcised before being admitted to the kingdom, that would have been the equivalent of declaring that Messiah's atonement was insufficient to save men with foreskins. If they were compelled to undergo a conversion to Judaism, the implication would be that Messiah was unable to save Gentiles.

PAUL RESPONDS

Paul responded to the Galatians by saying, "Are you so foolish? After beginning with the Spirit, are you now trying to attain your goal by human effort?"[146] The specific human effort Paul was speaking of was a legal conversion to Judaism through the rite of circumcision. In the eyes of men, circumcision allowed for a conventional, physical, human position in Israel. It was a position attained through natural, physical, human methods. Paul asked the Galatians, "Are you now trying to attain your goal by human effort? By natural means? Are you trying to buy your way into the kingdom by converting to Judaism?"

Paul's letter to the Galatians is a fierce, impassioned argument against the requirement of Gentile conversion. Paul contended that it was not necessary for Gentiles to convert to Judaism in order to be a legitimate part of the people of God. Gentiles did not need to be legally reckoned as part of the physical seed of Abraham (i.e., Jewish), because the promise of the covenant of the seed of Abraham had already received its ultimate fulfillment in the one singular seed, namely, Yeshua.

In Galatians 3:16 Paul wrote, "The promises [given to Abraham] were spoken to Abraham and to his seed. The Scripture does not say 'and to seeds,' meaning many people, but 'and to your seed,' meaning one person, who is Messiah." This means that the receiving of the promises given to Abraham is not based exclusively upon an individual being of the physical seed of Abraham. After all, Paul argues, the promise was not given to "seeds." "Seeds" in the plural form would suggest the many physical descendants of Abraham. Rather, he says, it was given to a singular seed. The singular "seed" of Abraham is Messiah. According to Paul, Messiah is the seed of Abraham. Yeshua is the promised seed and the fulfillment of the seed promises of the Scripture. Because of that, when Gentiles (those not of Abraham's seed) place faith in Messiah, the seed of Abraham, they are spiritually connected to that seed. To Paul, the passages and prophecies that speak about Abraham's seed blessing all nations, the seed of Israel becoming a community of nations, and the seed of Ephraim and Manasseh becoming a fullness of nations, are all ultimately fulfilled in the one seed that is Messiah.

From Paul's vantage point, for a Gentile believer to legally convert to Judaism was redundant. It was, if anything, an affront to Messiah because it implied that faith in Messiah was not adequate to secure a position within the people of God. It was a denial of the gospel. Paul says, "If you allow yourselves to be circumcised [that is, to undergo a formal conversion into Judaism as a necessary component of your salvation], Messiah is of no value to you." [147]

Messiah is of no value because the convert has opted to attain his participation in Israel through his own physical efforts. To Paul's way of thinking, ritual conversion after salvation is like campaigning for an office for which you have already been elected.

Paul responded to the bid for Gentile conversion to Judaism by forbidding the Galatians to circumcise. He may have even gone so far as to discourage all Gentile believers from circumcision as long as the commandment of circumcision was being misunderstood as the ticket into the kingdom.[148] In the case of Gentiles with authentic Jewish heritage, however, he did not hesitate to circumcise. Paul personally oversaw Timothy's circumcision.

MISREADING PAUL

Paul goes on to develop this argument from several angles. Later readers of the epistle who were not aware of the contextual situation interpreted Galatians as an anti-Torah and anti-Jewish work. Based largely on this misreading of Galatians, early Christianity jettisoned Torah and our connections to Judaism. We began to believe that anyone who attempted to keep a commandment of Torah was under the curse of the Torah. In retrospect, it was an absurd proposition, but to those who expounded the idea, it was consistent with their misreading of Galatians.

Paul was not preaching against Gentiles keeping the Torah. Technically, he was not even preaching against Gentiles becoming circumcised. He was preaching against Gentiles undergoing the conventional conversion into Judaism in order to achieve salvation and status in the Jewish community.

It would appear that the epistle to the Galatians was misunderstood even in Paul's own lifetime. When he arrived at Jerusalem in Acts 21, James warned him that there were false rumors going around to the effect that Paul was teaching "the Jews who live among the Gentiles to turn away from Moses, telling them not to circumcise their children."[149] Acts 21 makes clear that the rumors were false, but it shows how Paul's arguments concerning circumcision were already being misunderstood and misused.

Peter took note of people misunderstanding Paul. He said, "Paul's letters contain some things that are hard to understand, which ignorant and unstable people distort, as they do the other

Scriptures, to their own destruction" (2 Peter 3:16). If sorting out Paul's arguments was difficult for the first-century believers, how much more so for later generations? When the epistle is removed from the argument about conversion, one can hardly wonder that we misunderstood.

Ironically, the epistle to the Galatians is the very scripture that Christians most often use to refute Gentile believers who are beginning to return to their Jewish roots and practice aspects of Messianic Judaism. As Christians begin to involve themselves in the various aspects of biblical heritage (such as Sabbath observance, kosher laws, daily prayer, etc.), they are often rebuked by other believers quoting from Galatians. That is turning it exactly backward. Galatians was written to argue for Gentile inclusion in Israel, not Gentile exclusion from Israel.

ABRAHAM OUR FATHER

One of the angles of argument Paul developed was the Gentile believer's connection to the patriarchs. In Galatians, he claimed that all who place faith in Messiah become spiritual sons and daughters of Abraham. Years later, Paul reworked that thesis in the fourth chapter of his epistle to the Romans. In far more eloquent and measured terms, he stated that just as Abraham was credited with righteousness before he was circumcised, so too the Gentile believers are credited with righteousness apart from any legal conversion to Judaism. Therefore, Abraham is the "father of all who believe" so that the "promise may be guaranteed to all Abraham's seed—not only to those who are legally the seed of Abraham (i.e., ethnic Israelites and converts to Judaism), but also to those who are of the faith of Abraham. He is the father of all."[150]

Almost one thousand years later, Moses Maimonides found himself fighting the same kinds of battles Paul of Tarsus once fought in Galatians and Romans. In his day, a dispute had arisen among the Jewish communities about proselytes. Could a proselyte pray the *Amidah*? Could a former Gentile really say the words, "Blessed are you LORD, our God, God of *our* fathers, God of Abraham, God of Isaac, God of Jacob"? Some felt that such a prayer should be reserved only for the legitimate heirs of the patriarchs and that it was inappropriate for converts to Judaism to say those words. Maimonides responded as follows:

> Anyone who becomes a convert throughout the generations and anyone who unifies the Name of the Holy One as it is written in the Torah is a disciple of our father Abraham, and all of them are members of his household ... Hence you may say: "Our God and God of our fathers," for Abraham, peace be upon him, is your father ... Because you have come beneath the wings of the Divine Presence and attached yourself to God, there is no difference between us and you ... You certainly may recite the blessings, 'Who has chosen us,' 'Who has given us,' 'Who has caused us to inherit,' and 'Who has separated us,' for the Creator has already chosen you and has separated you from the nations and has given you the Torah."[151]

Maimonides's conclusion was not far removed from Paul's. As disciples of our father Abraham, following after the faith of Abraham, Gentile believers have the privilege to say, "Abraham our father." For there is neither Jew nor Gentile, slave nor free, male nor female, for we are all one in Messiah Yeshua.[152]

Gentile Israel

An even greater irony is that while the Jewish people are so often hated, reviled, and persecuted, there are many groups of people trying to claim that they are Israelites. Historically, Christianity has taught replacement theology—the belief that God divorced Israel and married the church. Gentile Christians then became the new Israel, the new people of God, while the Jews were left pathetic and unwanted, outside of God's covenant. In this traditional Christian worldview, we Gentile Christians become the inheritors of the promises of God while the Jews inherit eternal punishment.

Christianity was not the first religion to introduce replacement theology. The Samaritans had a head start on us by almost seven hundred years. Samaritans are actual descendants of the ten northern tribes. When the northern tribes were deported, and foreign populations were imported by Assyria, the resulting conglomeration of bloodlines and religions became the Samaritans. They were not quite Israelites, but not quite Gentiles either. They wrongly came to believe that they were the real and true Israel. (Coincidentally, they called themselves the "House of Joseph," as do some sectors of today's Two-House movement.) Josephus writes about them as follows, but his description could be applied to countless other sects and religions muscling in on Israel's identity:

> And when they see the Jews in prosperity, they pretend that they are changed, and allied to them, and call them kinsmen, as though they were derived from Joseph, and had by that means an original alliance with them; but when they see them falling into a low condition, they say they are no way related to them, and that the Jews have no right to expect any kindness or marks of family from them, but they declare that they are sojourners, that come from other countries. (*Antiquities* 9.14.3)

Why I Am of the Seed of Abraham

The best we can determine from the historical record is that the Galatians were originally Celtic people. The Celts are my forebears because my mother was a Kelly, an Irishwoman. As much as I might fancy being a physical descendant of Abraham, Isaac, and Jacob, the reality is that I, like the Galatians, am a descendant of the Celtic peoples.

My ancestors were not Israelites. They were wild people who worshipped cruel gods, gods that demanded human sacrifices and human blood. Their priests were called "druids"—mysterious men and women who communed with nature and the world of the spirits. The Celtic world was a world in between, a world on the edge of borders or across waters. My ancestors lived in fear of this shadowy world of malevolent spirits and bloodthirsty gods, of sacrifices on the equinox, of sacred stones and sacred trees. My ancestors ran naked on the battlefields, bodies painted with *woad*, shouting and screaming to terrify their enemies, then feasting on the blood of their victims. It's not a very pretty family portrait.

My claim to the inheritance of the kingdom and my place of standing in Israel is not based on my genetic descent. The truth that lays claim on me is much deeper, much more profound, and much more powerful than Israelite ancestry. I am part of the seed of Abraham because I am part of the body of Messiah, and Messiah is the seed of Abraham.

When a Gentile (or an Israelite, for that matter) places faith in Messiah, he becomes a part of the body of Messiah. Paul wrote, "Do you not know that your bodies are members of Messiah himself?"[153] The Master taught us that when we place our faith in him, we are in him and he in us. We are no longer ourselves alone, but we are invested with a share of his identity. His vivifying life force, even his very identity, is planted within us.

In the same mystical and inexplicable sense that he is one with the Father because he is in the Father and the Father is in him, so too we are made a part of this circle of unity when we come to faith.

Yeshua is Abraham's seed in a sense even more true and eternal than Isaac was. Yeshua is the ultimate fulfillment of those seed promises, and the promise is one of blessing for all nations in Abraham's seed. The Hebrew of Genesis 22:18 (and subsequent repetitions) uses the preposition *in*. All nations will be blessed *in* Abraham's seed.

How do we enter into Abraham's seed, especially if that seed is one man? We enter into the seed of Abraham when we enter into Messiah. Only in Messiah can one be truly in Abraham's seed.

The Master told us, "I am in my Father, and you are in me, and I am in you."[154] If we are in Messiah and he is in us, then we are in the seed of Abraham and the seed of Abraham is in us.

Paul said, "Therefore, if anyone is in Messiah, he is a new creation; the old has gone, the new has come."[155] My Gentile *ethnos* is no longer relevant as regards to my place in the family. If I accept those truths, then I am no longer in any need of clinging to replacement theology; I no longer need claim Israelite ancestry; I have no need to search for a Jew in my genealogy; I need not undergo a legal conversion to Judaism. To look for something more, something physical, something outside of my relationship with Messiah in order to offer me a sense of identity or status in the eyes of men is essentially the very sin the Galatians were committing.

Paul concludes his argument by saying, "Neither circumcision nor uncircumcision means anything; what counts is a new creation. Peace and mercy to all who follow this rule, even to the Israel of God." [156] When he says "circumcision," he means being legally Jewish, whether in the ethnic sense or the legal sense of a proselyte. When he says "uncircumcision," he means a Gentile who has not made a legal conversion to Judaism. When he says "new creation," he means Jews and Gentiles who belong to Messiah. When he says "Israel of God," he means all of us.

11

THE ETERNAL PURPOSE OF GOD

Ephesians 2

Far away, across many seas, down ancient roads and over steep hills is the place of God, the joy of the whole earth, the city of the Great King, Jerusalem. How many hands have been stretched out in prayer toward her walls? How many feet have walked the pilgrim miles to her gates? "I rejoiced with those who said to me, 'Let us go to the House of the LORD.' Our feet are standing in your gates, O Jerusalem." [157]

In the days of the apostles, the Temple of God was still in Jerusalem. Imagine our anticipation of the pilgrimage, our first sight of the Temple, our entrance through the city gates, our climb toward the Temple Mount. Immersed and purified, we are prepared to worship. Step by step, we climb the monumental stairway. It is a festival day. It is a time appointed to meet with the LORD. Our voices are joined with the voices of the other worshippers. We pass through the great gates and enter the court of the Gentiles. The House of God is before us now. We can see the smoke of the altar rising over the beautiful gate. We can catch the scent of the incense on the air. We can hear the song of the Levites. Our hearts are pounding within us. Since we first heard of him, we have longed for this moment. We mean to enter the House of God. We have come; we are here; we are with God's people; we are entering his House.

Then there is a wall—a partition made of stone—three cubits high. Spaced at equal intervals along the wall are pillars bearing inscriptions, some in Greek letters and some in Roman letters. These signs say that no foreigner should go within the sanctuary;[158] trespassers enter on the pain of death.[159]

We Gentiles may go no farther. We sons and daughters of the nations may look on the House of God, longing for the intimacy of his table, but we are on this side of the wall. His House, his people, even the blood atonement of his sacrifice are on the other side of the wall. The inescapable conclusion is that we are on the outside.

It was this very wall the Apostle Paul was walking past when he was accosted by an angry mob. They were not angry with him for teaching the death and resurrection of Messiah; they were angry with him for teaching Gentile inclusion in Israel. They were angry with him for filling the synagogue with Gentiles and declaring that those Gentiles were joint heirs with Israel. How dare he disregard the dividing wall?

Not that he had actually brought Gentiles into the inner courts of the Temple. Worse than that: He had transgressed the metaphoric wall separating Israel from non-Israel. He had obscured the sharp lines of who was in and who was out. His disregard for the metaphoric wall between Jew and Gentile led to his arrest, imprisonment, and eventual trial in Rome.

Breaking Down the Wall: Ephesians 2:8–14

While imprisoned in Rome, Paul had time to muse over the meaning of the mystery of the gospel. To Paul, the mystery of the gospel was not the mysterious incarnation, death, and resurrection of Yeshua. The mystery was that the Gentiles had somehow been included in Israel. Somehow, the dividing wall had been broken down. These musings led him to write the epistle to the Ephesians.

As he wrote to the Ephesians, Paul was deliberately clear about our identity as Gentiles. He makes it obvious that we were excluded from Israel. He says, "You were separate from Messiah, excluded from citizenship in Israel and foreigners to the covenants of the promise."[160] We were foreigners to the covenants of Israel. We were without a claim to the covenants of the forefathers.

Subsequent to our salvation, however, there has been a change in our status. Paul says that, while we were formerly Gentiles, somehow, through some mystery, our identity has changed: "But now in the Messiah Yeshua you who once were far away have been brought near through the blood of the Messiah."[161] We who were once far away have been brought near. We have been brought into the commonwealth of Israel. A radical transformation has occurred.

This transformation is in many ways equivalent to the legal transformation that occurs when a Gentile passes through the ritual of becoming a proselyte to Judaism. Paul, however, was not speaking of Gentiles converting to become legally Jewish. He was making the point that the Gentile believers have received this new identity without a formal ritual conversion. "Not by works lest any man boast,"[162] he said, and by works he meant the conventional conversion ritual, complete with the works of circumcision, immersion, and sacrifice. Those are the "works" of the Pauline Epistles.

The conversion Paul was speaking of was "not by works," but "by grace … through faith."[163] It came by the grace of God bestowed simply and purely through faith in Yeshua. He went on to explain the mechanics of the process in Ephesians 2:14: "For he [Yeshua] himself is our peace, who has made the two one and has destroyed the barrier, the dividing wall of hostility."

The image of a dividing wall of hostility between Jew and Gentile is borrowed directly from the architecture of the Jerusalem Temple. Paul invoked the image of the wall of separation between the court of the Gentiles and the court of Israel. The wall of separation, which forbade Gentiles on pain of death from entering the court of Israel and the Temple of God, was a potent metaphor for the theological exclusion of Gentiles from Israel and the kingdom. According to Paul, the wall of separation—the barrier between the people of the nations and the people of God—is destroyed by Messiah.

As we study through Ephesians 2, it's worth taking a careful look at how the New International Version expresses some of these ideas. From my point of view, it seems that the NIV takes a curious turn. The central clause of the passage reads as follows:

> For he himself is our peace, who has made the two one and has destroyed the barrier, the dividing wall of hostility, by abolishing in his flesh the law with its commandments and regulations. (Ephesians 2:14–15)

The translators of the NIV, like most translators of English versions of the Bible, have rendered the Greek to say that not only did Messiah's death bring peace between Jew and Gentile, but it also abolished the Torah. How convenient! Not only do we Gentiles receive full rights of participation and citizenship in Israel, but we are scot-free from acting like it at all! In one quick action, Messiah erased both the distinction between Jews and Gentiles and the whole Torah of Moses. Never mind that business about "Do not think I have come to abolish the law"; we have the evidence right here in Ephesians. The Torah, with its commandments and regulations, has been abolished.

Such a passage would certainly seem to eliminate the need for Gentiles (or Jews, for that matter) to observe any of the Torah. Since Messiah has abolished the Law with its commandments and regulations, it would be superfluous for anyone to keep Sabbath, to keep kosher, or even to refrain from covetousness, adultery, or idolatry. Jew and Gentile are thus made alike on the basis that they seemingly have no obligations of identity of any kind. The practice of Messianic Judaism by either Jew or Gentile is utterly unnecessary since the Torah is abolished.

I understand the passage differently. I do not read it as stating that Messiah abolishes the Torah; rather, he abolishes the enmity engendered by Torah. For clarity, I believe it should read, "For he himself is our peace, who has made the two one and has destroyed the barrier, the dividing wall, by abolishing in his flesh the enmity."[164] Specification of the source of this enmity follows immediately: "the Torah with its commandments and regulations." It is the Torah's commandments and regulations that have caused the enmity between Jew and Gentile.

The Torah does engender enmity between Israelite and Gentile, and the enmity is this: Israel is God's chosen and redeemed people, and the Gentiles are not. Israel is in covenant with the Father, and the Gentiles are not. Every command and ordinance given to Israel marked out the parameters of who Israel was and who Israel was not. The Torah determined who was in and who was out. The commandments are directed to the children of Israel, not to the children of Adam. The Torah itself is the wall of separation that keeps Jews and Gentiles separate.

According to Paul, the aspect of Torah that Messiah abolished was the separation between Jew and Gentile. It was abolished in the sense that Messiah has brought Gentile believers into the commonwealth of Israel. He seats them at the table with Israel and invites them to be partakers in the new covenant with Israel. Messiah bids the Gentiles to come and join themselves to the people of Israel. Because of the inclusion of Gentile believers in the greater people of Israel, the Torah is no longer a wall of separation, because it is no longer the criteria for defining the people of God. Moreover, in Messiah, Gentile believers have the prerogative to take hold of the covenant and take on the commandments. The enmity that kept Jews and Gentiles on opposite sides of the Torah wall has been removed.

Therefore, Ephesians 2:14–15 is not a contradiction of the Master's words in Matthew 5:17 ("Do not think I have come to abolish the Torah"), nor is it a textual justification to sin and sin boldly. Instead, it shows us how Gentiles are able to retain their Gentile identity while at the same time being regarded as part of Israel. "For he himself is our peace."

The Temple of the Future: Ephesians 2:14–15

In first-century Judaism, the dividing wall of hostility was more than just a metaphor. It was a literal wall in the Temple's outer courts that kept Gentiles at a distance. In the messianic era, there will be no wall of division in the Temple.

The prophet Isaiah declares that the stranger who keeps the Sabbath and holds fast to God's covenant will be received in the innermost courts of the Temple. His sacrifices will be received on the altar, and the Temple will be a house of prayer for Gentiles from every nation. Paul probably had this passage in mind as he wrote of Messiah abolishing the dividing wall. The dividing wall, which would forbid the Gentile from entering the Temple to offer sacrifice, is completely absent in Isaiah's messianic-age prophecy:

> And foreigners who bind themselves to the LORD to serve him, to love the Name of the LORD, and to worship him, all who keep the Sabbath without desecrating it and who hold fast to my covenant—these I will bring to my holy mountain and give them joy in my house of prayer. Their burnt offerings and sacrifices will be accepted on my altar; for my house will be called a house of prayer for all nations. (Isaiah 56:6–7)

Because the enmity has been abolished, Gentiles need not find a genetic justification for keeping the laws and ordinances of Torah, nor must they make a formal conversion to become Jewish. The dividing wall has been removed. Gentiles are free to move from the metaphoric court of the Gentiles into the metaphoric court of Israel. Within those courts, they are given free access to the Torah life that identifies Israel; they are given access to the House of God.

ONE NEW MAN: EPHESIANS 2:15–22

Paul goes on to say that Messiah's purpose was to create in himself one new man out of Jew and Gentile. The hostility between Jewish identity and Gentile identity was eliminated through the cross. Messiah preached the gospel of peace "to those who were far away" (i.e., Gentiles) and "to those who were near," (i.e., Jews).[165] The result of the gospel is that Gentiles "are no longer foreigners and aliens, but fellow citizens with God's people."[166]

Paul called himself the apostle to the Gentiles—the apostle to those who are strangers and aliens to God's people Israel. The good news is that through Messiah, we are strangers and aliens no more. We who were far away have been brought near. We who had no share or claim in Israel have been granted the status of citizenship in the commonwealth of Israel. We are citizens of Israel through

Messiah. This is not just symbolic status. This is a real position in and among the people of God.

Paul never makes an argument for Israel's inclusion in the church. Israel is not being joined to the church. The gospel does not make Jews into Gentiles. Paul's theology has Gentiles entering Kingdom Israel, joining with Israel as fellow citizens. We are strangers brought near; we are Israel by faith.

Jew and Gentile are joined together, like the two halves of Ezekiel's stick,[167] to make one new man. Paul compares this process to the bringing together of various building materials in order to make a holy temple for the LORD to reside in. He says, "In him [Messiah] the whole building is joined together and rises to become a holy temple in the Lord. And in him you too are being built together to become a dwelling in which God lives by his Spirit."[168] Paul means to tell us that not only has the metaphoric dividing wall that once forbade us from entering the Temple been broken, but along with Israel, we are being made into a spiritual temple for God to reside within. Gentile believers are being built together with Jewish believers into an eternal Temple.

THE ETERNAL PURPOSE OF GOD: EPHESIANS 3:1–9

Paul's radical theology of Gentile inclusion was not a popular one. Paul told the Ephesians that he was in prison "for the sake of you Gentiles."[169] His arrest in Jerusalem was a direct result of his mission to the Gentiles. In Ephesians 3, he explained to the Ephesians that he was the warden of something he called the "mystery of Messiah, a 'mystery made known to [Paul] by revelation.'"[170] What was Paul's big mystery? That Gentiles are heirs together with Israel:

> This mystery is that through the gospel the Gentiles are
> heirs together with Israel, members together of one body,
> and sharers together in the promise in Messiah Yeshua.
> (Ephesians 3:6)

It may sound somewhat matter-of-fact for us now, but it was a shock to first-century Jewish believers, even as it remains a shock to many Messianic Jewish leaders today. It is a staggering proposition. How can Israel be open to all nations and still retain her integrity as a people set apart and holy? Isn't that a contradiction?

How can Israel be the chosen people if everyone has a free ticket to be part of Israel?

It is a mystery that demands an explanation. It seems so irrational. What's the point of calling out a separate people from the nations if you intend to allow all nations to be a part of that people? Where's the sense in it? What might God intend to accomplish by extending the tent of Israel to encompass all nations?

The truly mysterious part of the Gentile inclusion is that it is "according to [God's] eternal purpose."[171] The "eternal purpose of God." Those are big words. Paul's premise is that the Gentile inclusion, which constitutes the mystery of Messiah, is according to the eternal purpose of God. He explains it in Ephesians 3:10, where he says, "[God's] intent was that now, through the Assembly (i.e., the body of believers in the Messiah), the manifold wisdom of God should be made known to the rulers and authorities in the heavenly realms."

Paul was saying that, through Messiah, God was in the business of saving human souls. When the LORD takes Gentile people away from their pagan gods, there is nothing that the "rulers and authorities in the heavenly realms"[172] can do about it. When God takes the children of clan Kelly away from the pagan gods of the Celts, when he takes the house of Lancaster away from the warrior gods of the Saxons, and when he redeems me and my family through Messiah, he is making a mockery of the demonic rulers and authorities of this world. Every Gentile who is taken from the false gods of the world and joined to the people of Israel represents a loss of territory and prestige for the enemy. That is the manifold wisdom of God.

It is a plan of universal dominion, a plan by which God intends to take over the world. Gentile believers are God's tokens of victory in an ancient struggle against darkness. The eternal purpose of God is the redemption of the whole world.

Paul's words are not unlike the passage from Deuteronomy in which Moses reminds Israel of the supremacy of the LORD over all the other gods:

> Has any god ever tried to take for himself one nation out
> of another nation, by testings, by miraculous signs and
> wonders, by war, by a mighty hand and an outstretched

arm, or by great and awesome deeds, like all the things the LORD your God did for you in Egypt before your very eyes? You were shown these things so that you might know that the LORD is God; besides him there is no other. (Deuteronomy 4:34–35)

The exodus from Egypt set the pattern. It was just the beginning. When God took the Israelites out of Egypt and away from Pharaoh and the gods of Egypt, he established his superiority over all those gods. Israel was his trophy of victory. He used the exodus from Egypt to establish his Name. The exodus from Egypt foreshadowed a second, greater exodus—an exodus begun under the blood of a greater Lamb. This second exodus is the redemption of the nations. As he redeems the Gentiles and joins them to his covenant people, God is repeating the exodus from Egypt over and over again, and there is nothing Pharaoh or the gods of Egypt can do about it. The spiritual powers and principalities of the Gentile nations can only watch in dismay as their brick-makers join themselves to Israel and slip away through the Red Sea.

Our salvation is a demonstration of God's wisdom and sovereign power to rulers and authorities in the heavenly realms. What other god has ever tried to take for himself one nation out of every nation? Which god of the nations has done anything like it? Which god of the nations can do anything to stop it? To Paul, the mystery of the gospel is the salvation of the whole world.

The picture is much bigger than just me and my personal salvation. It is bigger than the liberation from Egypt. It is bigger than the salvation of Judah. It is bigger than the return of the ten lost tribes. God's eternal purpose is that his wisdom should be made known to the rulers and authorities in heavenly realms by means of taking away their people and their property, and by means of redeeming a people out of every tribe, tongue, and nation on earth.

It was for this mystery that Paul was willing to be held in chains.

Too Small a Thing

Isaiah spoke of this mystery.

In a vision recorded in his book of comfort, Isaiah saw the LORD speaking to his servant the Messiah. The LORD said to his servant, "It is too small a thing for you to be my servant to restore the tribes of Jacob and bring back those of Israel I have kept. I will also make you a light for the Gentiles, that you may bring my salvation to the ends of the earth."[173]

The scope of Messiah's work is not limited to the restoration of the tribes of Israel. That purpose is too small when compared with the greater purpose God has in mind. The eternal purpose of God is that Messiah should carry the LORD's salvation to the Gentiles, even to the ends of the earth.

The Gentiles Isaiah spoke of are the same Gentiles Paul was writing about in the book of Ephesians. They are those who were strangers and aliens, those who were far off, strangers to the promises, without God and without hope. They are the "foreskinned," the nations, the *ethnos*. They are the ones upon whom God intends to shine the light of Messiah. This is in keeping with God's eternal purpose, that the manifold wisdom of God should be made known to the rulers and authorities in the heavenly realms. God's salvation must go to the ends of the earth. All nations will be blessed.

The eternal purpose of God culminates in a scene from the book of Revelation. John looks and sees "a great multitude, which no man could number, of all nations, and kindreds, and people, and tongues, [standing] before the throne, and before the Lamb."[174] This great, innumerable multitude is contrasted with the numerable 144,000 from the twelve tribes. The point of the passage is that God's salvation is universal and includes a Gentile majority from every ethnicity.

THE ISRAEL OF GOD

Gentile believers have a legitimate place in the Israel of God. We have a place more secure than even Jewish (or Israelite) ancestry or a conversion ritual could ever offer us. Our place is secured by the blood of Messiah and foreordained by the eternal purpose of God. We have an identity in Kingdom Israel among the people of God. Just as Abraham believed by faith and it was credited to him as righteousness—before he was circumcised—we have a place in the Israel of God. Just as he brought near those who were far off, we have been brought near through Messiah and given a place in the commonwealth of Israel. Just as Ruth was compared to a goodly branch grafted into Abraham's tree, we have been grafted into the Israel of God. Just as Joseph married Asenath—the pagan, Gentile daughter of an Egyptian priest—so too we have been granted a place in Kingdom Israel by virtue of our husband. Just as Jacob adopted Ephraim and Manasseh as his own, giving them a place among the tribes and the sons of Israel, so too our Father in heaven has adopted us into his people, along with his chosen people, the children of Jacob. Just as the Hebrews passed through the Red Sea like converts passing through an immersion, we have been born again of an imperishable seed. We are new creations. We are the sheep not of the sheepfold that the Good Shepherd brings and joins to his flock Israel. Just as Israel was betrothed by God to be his special treasure, a kingdom of priests and a holy nation, so we have been joined to the bride and given a place in the Israel of God. Just as the voice of God at Sinai spoke in the languages of every nation and the Spirit spoke through the believers in the languages of every nation at Pentecost, we of every nation have heard the voice and followed. Just as the Galatians and the Ephesians were made sons of Abraham by faith in the seed of Abraham, we have been given a place at the table with our father Abraham. Just as John saw a mighty throng, a great multitude, which no man could number, of all nations and kindreds and people and tongues, standing before the throne, we have a place in Israel.

Epilogue
Journey to Jerusalem

The ancient prophets tell us that in the messianic age to come, we will find ourselves making pilgrimage to Jerusalem. In a sense, we are already on the journey. To help guide us along the way, the prophets of Israel give us glimpses of our destination and destiny. According to the prophets, we are going to messianic Jerusalem. We are going up to the city of the Great King.

Keeping this goal in clear view makes it easier to understand the journey. Our final destination is Jerusalem and the service of the King.

Isaiah Sees the Future

The prophet Isaiah paints an especially vivid picture of our pilgrimage. He foresaw all nations making pilgrimage to Jerusalem. He tells us that in the messianic age, the Temple in Jerusalem will be the chief place of worship. All nations will ascend to it. In Jerusalem, all nations will learn the ways of Torah. The result will be universal peace:

> In the last days the mountain of the LORD's Temple will be established as chief among the mountains; it will be raised above the hills, and all nations will stream to it. Many peoples will come and say, "Come, let us go up to the mountain of the LORD, to the house of the God of Jacob. He will teach us his ways, so that we may walk in his paths." The law will go out from Zion, the word of the LORD from Jerusalem. He will judge between the nations and will settle disputes for many peoples. They will beat

their swords into plowshares and their spears into pruning hooks. Nation will not take up sword against nation, nor will they train for war anymore. (Isaiah 2:2–4)

Isaiah tells us that God intends to bring all peoples into his kingdom. Messiah himself will be like "a banner for the peoples, the nations will rally to him, and his place of rest will be glorious."[175] His place of rest is messianic Jerusalem.

Through the prophet Isaiah, the spirit of Messiah declares, "The Torah will go out from me; my justice will become a light to the nations … my arm will bring justice to the nations."[176] Isaiah tells us that the nations will keep the Sabbath. The nations will keep the covenant of Torah. Their burnt offerings and sacrifices will be accepted on the LORD's altar. The Temple in Jerusalem "will be called a house of prayer for all nations."[177] As the nations ascend to Jerusalem, they will bring the exiles of Israel with them.[178] Together, Jew and Gentile will worship before the LORD on the monthly new moons and the weekly Sabbaths:

> "From one new moon to another and from one Sabbath to another, all mankind will come and bow down before me," says the LORD. (Isaiah 66:23)

Observing the new moons means that all mankind will keep the biblical calendar. Observing the weekly Sabbath means that all mankind will keep the covenant sign of Israel.[179]

PEEKING AT THE KINGDOM

The mystery of the gospel is the inclusion of the Gentiles into the people of God, the grafting into Israel. The eternal purpose of God is nothing less than the redemption of the whole creation. Messiah accomplishes both. In the messianic age to come, he will subdue all nations and make all mankind subject to the good and perfect Law of God. Messiah's kingdom is the destination of the journey.

As the prophet Isaiah described the great pilgrimage ascending to messianic Jerusalem, he saw that the pilgrims were not just Israelites. Among the multitudes ascending to the Holy City, he saw strangers, foreigners, and people of other nations. He cried out to Jerusalem, "Nations will come to your light, and kings to the brightness of your dawn. Lift up your eyes and look about you: all assemble and come to you; your sons come from afar, and your daughters are carried on the arm."[180]

And as the rivers of pilgrims from every tribe, tongue, and nation on earth approach the Holy City, Isaiah cries out to them: "Pass through, pass through the gates! Prepare the way for the people. Build up, build up the highway! Remove the stones. Raise a banner for the nations."[181] He welcomes the pilgrims into the gates of Jerusalem.

THE ROAD TO JERUSALEM

All nations will ascend to Jerusalem to worship the King, learn his Law (Torah), and keep his commandments. Messianic Jerusalem is the destination. In that day, the whole world will be keeping the Torah. All nations will make pilgrimage to Jerusalem, because Jerusalem will be the capital city of all nations. The kingdom of Israel will be universal. All men will serve the king of Israel according to the Torah of Israel. That is the destination; that is the goal.

Knowing that we will all be keeping the biblical calendar in Messiah's kingdom makes it clear that keeping the calendar is part of kingdom living. In that day, all mankind will keep the seventh-day, biblical Sabbath. When we sit down to eat with the Master, the only menu options will be kosher.

In that day, all nations will keep Torah. The Torah shall go forth from Zion, a light to all nations and a law to all men. If the Torah is the law of the kingdom, shouldn't all the subjects of the king obey that law? If messianic Jerusalem is our final destination, shouldn't we turn our hearts toward her now? We don't have to wait until we arrive in her gates; we can begin the celebration right now.

APPENDIX ONE
THE SOREG

In the course of his massive remodeling of the Jerusalem Temple, King Herod extended the Temple Mount significantly by constructing a retaining wall and adding fill.

Prior to Herod's additions, the original Temple Mount platform was marked off by a balustrade of stone latticework (*soreg*). The balustrade was designed to maintain the original dimensions of the Temple area—and to keep non-Jews out. Second Temple Judaism regarded that original area as sacrosanct to Jews alone.

The Mishnah, in *Middot* 2:3, reports the *soreg* as 10 handbreadths high. Josephus recalls it as a slightly taller 3 cubits. So it was approximately four feet in height. The courtyard outside of this barrier was referred to as the Court of the Gentiles. Plaques were posted on the balustrade forbidding Gentiles to go beyond it. Josephus, an eye-witness to the Temple, describes the barrier as follows:

> There was a partition made of stone all around, whose height was three cubits; its construction was very elegant; upon it stood pillars, at equal distances from one another, declaring the law of purity, some in Greek, and some in Roman letters, that "no foreigner should go within that sanctuary." (*Jewish War* 5:5:2)

> Thus was the first enclosure. In the midst of which, and not far from it, was the second, to be gone up to by a few steps: this was encompassed by a stone wall for a partition, with an inscription, which forbade any foreigner to go in under pain of death. (*Antiquities* 15:11:5)

Up until the late 19th century, this dividing wall was known to us only from the ancient sources mentioned above. Then, during Clermont and Ganneau's 1871 excavations of Jerusalem, a stone plaque was discovered. It apparently came from the original dividing wall and bears the complete Greek text. The plaque now resides in the Istanbul Museum.

The inscription reads: "No foreigner is to enter within the balustrade and enclosure around the Temple area. Whoever is caught will have himself to blame for his death which will follow." Incredibly, in 1936, another such inscription was unearthed near Jerusalem's Lion Gate. The second inscription was only partially preserved. Both inscriptions are pictured here.

(Photos from JUC field book, Istanbul Museum, and Israel Museum, respectively. No credits given.)

MHΔENAΛΛOΓENHEIΣΠO
ΡΕΥΕΣΟΛΙΕΝΤΟΣΤΟΙΠΕ
ΡLTOIEPONTPYΦAKTOYKAI
ΠΕΡΙΒΟΛΟΥΟΣΔΑΝΛΗ
ΦΘΗΕΑΥΤΩΙΑΙΤΙΟΣΕΣ
ΤΑΙΔΙΑΤΟΕΞΛΚΟΛΟΥ
ΟΕΙΝΟΑΝΑΤΟΝ

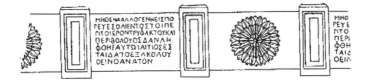

NO FOREIGNER IS TO EN-
TER WITHIN THE BALUS-
TRADE AND ENCLOSURE AROUND
THE TEMPLE AREA. WHOEVER IS
CAUGHT WILL HAVE HIMSELF TO
BLAME FOR HIS DEATH WHICH
WILL FOLLOW.

WE WERE IN A SYNAGOGUE

A Sabbath lecture presented at Messianic Synagogue Beth Immanuel in Hudson, WI, as part of the 2008 First Fruits of Zion national Shavuot conference. All Scripture quotations are from the English Standard Version.

When the day of Pentecost arrived, they were all together in one place. (Acts 2:1)

We are back. After a long road, we have returned. Through different paths and different journeys, we have come together and come to the same place to keep the holy Sabbath in obedience to the commandment of God and to the glory of the God and Father of our Lord Yeshua the Messiah, to whom belongs all glory, splendor, praise, and adoration from now and until forever, amen.

"Shabbat Shalom" is the theme of this year's conference. "Shabbat Shalom" means "Sabbath Peace," and it is our desire at First Fruits of Zion to invite everyone into the peace of the Sabbath today, to let it wash over you, that you might lay your burdens down at the foot of the cross of Messiah and let the peace of God, which passes all understanding, hold you in its sway.

"Shabbat Shalom" is not just a greeting; it is a state of being. It is one that used to be an important part of the weekly routine for all disciples of Yeshua, those early generations, the apostolic-era believers, who week after week kept the Shabbat and attended the synagogue on Shabbat.

The Sabbath

The Sabbath is certainly the star attraction of Messianic Judaism. It is our magnet. It is the easiest gimmick we have. We can reach into our bag of tricks and pull it out and say, "Hey, we got Sabbath; do you?" And we draw people from all different backgrounds, oftentimes primarily because we are Sabbath observant, and many believers are looking for some place to keep the Sabbath.

However, this is not always a good thing. I believe we need our congregations and communities to get past being a repository for disgruntled Sabbatarian Christians with no place better to go. Messianic Judaism is not just another denominational flavor in the church that happens to meet on Saturday. A congregation like Beth Immanuel is a Messianic synagogue.

And if you are a believer in Yeshua, regardless of what type of Christian you are, when you step into a Messianic synagogue, you should be greeted with the words "Shabbat Shalom; welcome home."

Even if you are a stranger (and there are many strangers with us here today), even if you have never been in a Messianic synagogue before, you should be greeted with the words "Welcome home." The synagogue is the home from which we all came, and now we are returning home. You have come home. Welcome home.

The Synagogue

Writing to the believers, James the brother of the Master said, "For if a man wearing a gold ring and fine clothing comes into your [synagogue], and a poor man in shabby clothing also comes in …" (James 2:2), and then he warned us not to treat one man partially, above the other. But today, I want you to notice that in James 2:2, the apostle uses the word *synagogue*. Our English Bibles tend to translate it as "assembly" in order to avoid the obvious and unpleasant implication that believers were meeting in synagogues, but the Greek says, "If a man comes into your synagogue."

We were in a synagogue.

In Acts 15, when the apostles gave the Gentiles the four essentials, they explained that the Torah was heard every week in the synagogues. They obviously expected us to hear it there because we were in the synagogues. Paul always went to the synagogues, and almost all of his converts were Jews and Gentiles who were attending synagogues and continued to attend synagogues so long as they were able. We were in the synagogues.

Whenever the Master entered a village, he drew a large crowd. Many gathered to hear his teaching and to see his miracles. The Gospels say that "Jesus went throughout all the cities and villages, teaching in their synagogues" (Matthew 9:35), that "He went throughout all Galilee, teaching in their synagogues" (Matthew 4:23), that "He was preaching in the synagogues of Judea" (Luke 4:44), that "Again he entered the synagogue" (Mark 3:1), that "On the Sabbath he began to teach in the synagogue, and many who heard him were astonished" (Mark 6:2), that "He was teaching in one of the synagogues on the Sabbath" (Luke 13:10), that "On another Sabbath, he entered the synagogue and was teaching" (Luke 6:6), and that the Master said, "I have spoken openly to the world. I have always taught in synagogues and in the temple, where all Jews come together. I have said nothing in secret" (John 18:20).

The Gospels are very clear about this matter: Yeshua was in the synagogue.

On Sabbath mornings, when Yeshua was in town, he attended the local synagogue. The synagogue officials and teachers probably yielded their pulpits to the visiting rabbi. After all, he was the one the people wanted to hear. He was the reason the crowd was there. Whenever Yeshua was in the synagogue, the building was packed.

CHURCH OF THE ANNUNCIATION

He did not just attend the synagogue; he participated in the Torah reading services. Luke 4:16 says, "And he came to Nazareth, where he had been brought up. And as was his custom, he went to the synagogue on the Sabbath day, and he stood up to read."

Last year, I went with several of my colleagues—Boaz Michael, Toby Janicki, and Joel Powell—to do some filming in Nazareth. We went to the Church of the Annunciation, the largest church in Israel—the largest church in the Middle East, actually. Underneath this beautiful Franciscan church is some amazing archaeology. The Franciscan archaeologists uncovered a crusader-era church, and that crusader era marks the place of a Byzantine-era church, and some remains are visible.[182] The Franciscan archaeologists say that in the stone work of the Byzantine-era church's foundations they discovered earlier stones in secondary use. These reused stones were characteristic of the type and cut of stones used in early Galilean synagogues. The accumulation of the evidence gives us every reason to believe that Church of the Annunciation marks the location of an early Nazareth synagogue, likely the synagogue in which the Master read Torah.

In later years, it may well have been attended by his clansmen and family members, because Nazareth became a center of believing Davidians devoted to their famous cousin.[183] But in the Byzantine era the synagogue was replaced with a church.

King David's Tomb

Another place we visited was King David's tomb on Mount Zion in Jerusalem. It functions as a sort of synagogue, *beit midrash* ("house of study"), and holy place all at once. People come there to pray and study. Carved into the Hadrianic-era stones is a large niche, like a small apse, in which the Torah scrolls are kept. The archaeology of King David's tomb is very intriguing. In Christian tradition, it is supposed to mark the place of the Last Supper. During the crusader era, the crusaders built much of the currently existing structure, but they also spuriously identified it with King David, and that is why it is today considered to be the tomb of King David. But before it was a crusader shrine, it was a Byzantine-era church commemorating the place of the upper room, where the Last Seder took place, and in Christian tradition, the place where the Holy Spirit was poured out on the believers on the Day of Pentecost.

Why did the Byzantines suppose that this location was the place of the upper room? Because they built their church on top of what literary sources and archaeological evidence suggest was a synagogue.[184] According to some old church sources, it was the synagogue of the Jewish believers who returned to Jerusalem from Pella three years after the destruction of Jerusalem.[185] Indeed, several of the stones in the lower courses of the building are Herodian-era stones in secondary use, and archaeologists date some of them to the era of just after the destruction of the Temple and Jerusalem.

Some even suggest that the stone apse where the Torah scrolls are kept today might have originally been the sacred niche in which those early Jewish believers stored their sacred scrolls.[186]

To recapitulate: According to the legend, the early Jewish believers returning from Pella after the destruction of the Temple built a synagogue on the spot where the upper room of the Last Seder once occurred. This synagogue remained in the hands of the Jewish believers until it fell into the hands of Byzantines, who rebuilt it as a monumental church. Subsequently it was rebuilt by the crusaders, and today it is back in Jewish hands, revered as the tomb of King David.

Underneath all the layers, we were in a synagogue.

SYNAGOGUE OF THE CHRISTIANS

It is intriguing to me that in Antioch, where we were first called Christians, there was a large Jewish community with more than a dozen synagogues.[187] In those days each synagogue had a name, like "Synagogue of the Hebrews," "Synagogue of the Freedmen," or something to denote their particular sect. Sociologist, historian, and scholar Marcus Zetterholm, in his book *The Formation of Christianity in Antioch*, suggests that originally our synagogue in Antioch was called the Synagogue of the *Christianos*; i.e., the Synagogue of the Christians—or to put it in our English, the Synagogue of the Messianics.[188]

SYNAGOGUE OF CAPERNAUM

Whenever First Fruits of Zion takes a tour group to Israel, we always go to Capernaum, where the remains of a fourth-century synagogue have been partially reassembled by the Franciscans. It was a beautiful synagogue constructed of ornate limestone, but under the foundations of this beautiful, Byzantine-era synagogue are the simple black basalt foundation stones of a much older, first-century synagogue, the synagogue of Capernaum where Yeshua regularly taught and where he performed many of his miracles:

> And they went into Capernaum, and immediately on the Sabbath he entered the synagogue and was teaching. (Mark 1:21)

Jesus said these things in the synagogue, as he taught at Capernaum. (John 6:59)

Those black basalt foundation stones, those sacred stones, absorbed the sound of his voice as he taught, as he prayed, as he chanted the Torah in that synagogue. To me, they are the rocks that cry out.

RELIGIOUS ARCHAEOLOGY

I look at the situation of the Church of the Annunciation in Nazareth as a sort of metaphor for what we are doing in the Messianic movement. We are digging beneath the foundations of the church to discover the original structure, and when you dig beneath the church, at the foundations of Christianity, you find layer built upon layer stretching back through the centuries, until you reach the earliest archaeological level, and there you find the synagogue. That is why I am passionate about returning Messianic Judaism to an authentic synagogue service. Not because it's cool, not because it's elitist, and certainly not because it is popular and draws big crowds, but because it is authentic.

When we talk about incorporating synagogue liturgy, we are not talking about something new, like some spiritual fad. We are talking about something very old—the oldest thing. Messianic Judaism is not like dressing up and playing cowboy. Underneath all the layers, this is who we really are. It is real Christianity.

ANTIPATHY FOR JUDAISM

Luke 4:16 reminds us that it was the Master's custom to attend synagogue on the Sabbath and to participate in the public reading of the Torah and in the Sabbath prayers. Luke tells us that Yeshua "stood up to read," meaning he read from the Torah before the scroll of the prophet Isaiah was handed to him to read the *haftarah.*

Given that it was the Master's custom to attend the synagogue and participate in synagogue services every week, and given the fact that the early believers all met in synagogues, that the archaeology demonstrates that our places of worship were synagogues, that our liturgy was synagogue-based, and that we are now part of the Messianic Jewish movement (which ostensibly is supposed to be a restoration of the original church, back to the early believers)—given all of that, I find it terribly ironic that many practitioners of Messianic Judaism and people who call themselves Messianic have such a strong aversion to the synagogue mode of worship.

Here is the irony: If I were a Catholic, I would want to be Catholic and I would want to participate in mass. That's what Catholics do; it's part of being Catholic. I would not have to argue with other Catholics about what should constitute a legitimate Catholic mass. If I were Lutheran, I would want to have a Lutheran service and practice the things that Lutherans practice and pray the prayers that Lutherans pray, because that would be my religion. But for some reason, many people who claim to be Messianic harbor a deep resistance to the practice of Messianic Judaism. We harbor a suspicion and paranoia about too real and genuine an expression of Judaism. Dare I say, we harbor an antipathy for anything "too Jewish."

The matter is even stranger when we remember that, though being Catholic and being Lutheran are very worthy things, Yeshua and the original apostles were not Catholic; they did not attend mass. They were not Lutheran. They were Jewish, part of Judaism, and their religion—and the religion of all the early believers—was Judaism. I see it as ironic that, although we find loyal Lutherans who are committed followers of Yeshua and yet faithful to the Lutheran religion, and loyal Catholics who are devoted to Yeshua yet faithful to Catholicism, a Messianic who wants to follow Yeshua and practice a devout form of Messianic Judaism is challenged and opposed within Messianic Judaism.

EXILES FROM THE SYNAGOGUE

A look back at our history explains the matter. There is no need to speak of the *Birkat HaMinim*, the malediction against sectarians that was introduced to synagogues near the end of the first century with the purpose of forcing out sectarians, including believers. The Master had foreseen this. He told us, "They will put you out of the synagogues" (John 16:2).

We were put out of the synagogue. Like a child run out of his home by a wicked stepmother, we wandered out in the world for years. While on this long sojourn, the child grew and forgot his own name. He lodged in strange houses and learned new customs, acquired a wife and children, all the time living like an amnesiac who no longer knew the way back home. One day, quite by accident, he was traveling to a certain place when he recognized something familiar about the village through which the road was passing. Every corner seemed somehow familiar, yet strange and unknown at the same time. Then he saw the house he had once known as a child, so long forgotten. Stepping through the front door, he returned unrecognized and unrecognizing, but nonetheless knowing, "I once lived here. This was my home. This was my room. This was my family."

WHO ARE WE?

In Messianic Judaism, we often say, "Who are we? What do we call ourselves?" Perhaps there are some of us, who, like myself, find the term "Messianic Judaism" somewhat irksome at times and shy away from labeling ourselves as such. In that case, what should we call ourselves? The term "Messianic Jew" might work if you are Jewish, but it requires more explanation. Besides, that is now such a broad category that it fails to really describe what we are talking about. After all, most congregations that call themselves Messianic Jewish are merely practicing a cosmetic form of Messianic Judaism like the early missionary-outreach efforts. They may meet on Saturday, but not because they keep Sabbath. They blow a shofar, but not because it's Rosh HaShanah. They wear a prayer shawl and kippah (or at least the women do). To our sorrow, they serve unclean food and still repudiate the Torah as obsolete.

NEITHER FISH NOR FOWL

So then what are we? Neither fish nor fowl. And that is the problem. We do need a label, and the Messianic shoe fits, so I'm going to wear it, regardless of whether or not I like others with the same shoe size. This is who we are.

I still don't like the term "Messianic Judaism" because of some of its associations: the disingenuousness of its origins, being the missionary in disguise, and so forth. But it is the only term on the table. It is the best term there is to describe who we are. And we should not let people who disdain Judaism define the meaning of the term Messianic Judaism. We should define it ourselves. It is us; it is what we do, believing Jews and Gentiles who have opted to journey back to the religion of the apostles as a component of discipleship to Yeshua. I am a Messianic Gentile. I practice Messianic Judaism. I am a disciple of Yeshua of Nazareth.

This does not grant me status in the eyes of men. I have no halachic standing in Israel. But in the words of the apostle, "For his sake I have suffered the loss of all things and count them as rubbish, in order that I may gain Christ and be found in him, not having a righteousness of my own that comes from the law, but that which comes through faith in Christ" (Philippians 3:8–9). Our identity is in Messiah, in the eyes of God and not in the eyes of men. If we are seeking approval in the eyes of men, we are no longer seeking God's approval.

A Good Christian

The early believers had a similar identity problem. The book of Acts makes it clear that they were practicing Judaism. The apostles and the early believers, and even the Gentile believers, had formed a sect of Judaism. They called themselves or were called "the Way," "the Disciples," "the Sect of the Nazarenes" (by others), but the religion they were practicing was Judaism. Even the Gentiles among them were practicing Judaism, to whatever extent they felt compelled.

By the middle of the second century, at least two major groups had split off from that movement: the Nazarenes on the one hand and the Christians on the other hand. The Nazarenes, still practicing Judaism, were predominantly Jewish, while the Christians, no longer practicing Judaism, were predominantly Gentile. However, there were initially Gentile Nazarenes, and there were always Jewish Christians, so it went both ways. The division was not just ethnic.

The Nazarenes existed as an independent sect within Judaism, quite distinct from Christianity, until at least the third century. The church father Jerome knew Nazarenes and studied with them.[189] He copied down passages of their writings. The early church writer Epiphanius wrote extensively about their beliefs and practices, which he summed up by saying, "They differ from the Jews and Christians only in this and nothing else—with the Jews they do not agree because of their belief in Christ, with the Christians they disagree because of their practice of the Law, circumcision, Sabbath, and other things."[190]

They were Torah keepers, just like those zealous Jewish believers in the book of Acts. They practiced the religion of Yeshua: Judaism. They differed from the Jews in nothing except that they believed Jesus is the Messiah. That's who we were.

I want to be a good Christian. I believe that in order to be a truly biblical Christian, it helps to be practicing the same religion that biblical Christians practiced. In the days of the apostles, the religion we now recognize as Christianity had not yet developed.

A few years ago, we were having some carpeting installed at our house. I had a conversation with the carpet guy. He noticed a mezuzah on our door, several books in Hebrew lying about, etc., and he asked if we were Jewish. I said, "No, I'm a Christian, but I practice Judaism." He thought about that for three seconds, then his face lit up, and he said, "That makes total sense! After all, Jesus and the apostles were all Jewish." The carpet guy gets it. Why doesn't the Messianic Jewish movement get it?

What does it mean to be Messianic? It means you believe in Yeshua of Nazareth while practicing a form of Judaism. That's what First Fruits of Zion is all about. That is why a congregation like Beth Immanuel is here. That is what this conference is all about.

RESTORATION

A few years ago I wrote a book called *Restoration: Returning the Torah of God to the Disciples of Jesus*. It was a sustained argument for why Christianity should reconsider Torah and Judaism. The premise of the book was this: Yeshua, the apostles, and the first believers were Torah keeping. They practiced the Jewish religion, a religion called Judaism. Even the Gentile believers were plugged into this religion. But as time went on, a majority of Gentile believers left that practice and formed a new reactionary religion that came to be called Christianity. The new religion defined itself in antithesis to Judaism and Torah. It became, on many points, the opposite of the original faith.

Our great mission at First Fruits of Zion is to restore the original, to go back before the Protestant Reformation, before the Vatican, before the church councils, before Nicea, before Constantine, before Ignatius and the church fathers, all the way back to those original apostolic-era communities. As much as possible, I want to practice my faith as they did. I want to revive that, because that is as close to the actual faith, practice, and life of Yeshua as I can get. To me, that is the ideology that underlies Messianic Judaism.

Why should we go to all this bother? Because we are in love with Yeshua of Nazareth, and we know no better way to honor him than to walk as he walked, live as he lived, and even to worship as he worshipped in obedience to the Father, in the unity of the Spirit, in one accord with the people, even the people of God, the people of Israel.

The synagogue service we participated in this morning represents our return home. For the sake of Yeshua, for the sake of the apostles, for the sake of the early believers, for the sake of the Torah, for the sake of the future of Messianic Judaism, for our children, and for our grandchildren, we are endeavoring to leave a legacy for future generations, that they might not have to wander out in the world not knowing who they are and where they belong. We are striving that they might have a home back in the synagogue, in the midst of the fellowship of brothers and sisters, abounding in the love of Messiah and the common bond of the Holy Spirit.

We were in a synagogue, and today we are coming back to the synagogue, but even better than that, we are coming back to a Messianic synagogue. Welcome home.

TO PRAY AS A GENTILE

A lecture presented at Messianic Synagogue Beth Immanuel in Hudson, WI, as part of the 2008 First Fruits of Zion national Shavuot conference. All Scripture quotations are from the English Standard Version.

First Fruits of Zion has asked me to speak on the subject of controversial blessings that are found in the traditional synagogue liturgy. For this hour, I am going to be speaking about controversial prayers and blessings, not in the sense of the actual content of the blessing—that is not where the controversy lies—but in the sense of who the person praying the blessing is. In fact, a better title for this session might have been "Controversial Blessers." Even better yet, if I could offer a title for this lecture, I would base it on the title of that classic book by Rabbi Hayim Donin, *To Pray as Jew*, which was my first real introduction to Judaism proper. In the same vein, I'm giving this lecture the title "To Pray as a Gentile."

I can illustrate the controversial aspect of praying as a Gentile with the following anecdote. I once had a friend, a study partner of sorts, both of us Christians, both of us Gentiles, both studying a variety of subjects with Chabad Lubavitch and attending classes taught by some prominent, local, orthodox rabbis. On one occasion my friend plucked up his courage and asked the rabbi for permission to pray *shacharit* (the morning prayers) with the weekday minyan (prayer quorum) in the synagogue. The rabbi scrunched up his face and said, "Well, the problem is, the prayers don't really apply to you. They aren't appropriate for a Gentile."

That is often the impression that a Gentile gets as he approaches Jewish liturgy for the first time. In Messianic Judaism, this can be especially problematic in regard to the Sabbath prayers, because it is on the Sabbath that we are most likely to find ourselves in a mixed venue praying a common prayer, both Jew and Gentile together.

INAPPROPRIATE PRAYERS

To pray Jewish liturgy as a Gentile raises lots of problems and poses lots of questions, because the prayers, as they were formulated by the Jewish people, were not formulated with Gentiles—much less Gentile believers—in view. One may wonder if it is appropriate for a non-Jew to pray prayers like the *Kiddush*: "For you chose us and sanctified us from all of the peoples, and you caused us to inherit your holy Sabbath." It was the Jewish people who were chosen and set apart. Also problematic are the numerous references to "the God of our fathers." Can a Gentile refer to Abraham, Isaac, and Jacob as his fathers? Or, for example, consider the *Oseh Shalom* prayer, which says, "Make peace upon us and upon all Israel," where the person praying is declaring himself as part of the collective body of Israel. Or consider the request of the second blessing before the morning *Shema*, which says, "Cause us to walk independently into our land," when the land of Israel is surely given to the Jewish people and not to all nations. What about the frequently repeated liturgical formula "Who has sanctified us with his commandments and commanded us to …" Who did God sanctify with his commandments and to whom did he give the commandments? Surely it was Israel, the Jewish people.

Paul says that to the Jewish people "belong the adoption, the glory, the covenants, the giving of the law, the worship, and the promises. To them belong the patriarchs, and from their race, according to the flesh, is the Christ who is God over all, blessed forever. Amen" (Romans 9:4–5).

Unless a person obstinately insists that Paul was speaking halachically when he said, "There is neither Jew nor Greek,"[191] and, therefore, Greeks are Jews, the traditional Sabbath prayers of the *Siddur* (prayer book) would seem to create an insurmountable dividing wall of partition, a new *soreg*, between the Jewish believer in Yeshua and the Gentile believer.

One obvious solution would be to alleviate the discomfort by creating a separate set of prayers for Gentiles—a Gentile siddur, a separate Gentile prayer service, by and for Gentile believers. And that would be one approach. But this has already been done; it was done as early as the second century, and it is called Christianity.

Surely the apostles did not envision Jews and Gentiles being forced to worship in separate venues. Imagine the synagogue bisected by crossed walls dividing the congregation into four quadrants: a *mechitzah* ("partition") separating men and women, and both of those bisected by another wall separating Jews and Gentiles. A ridiculous proposition.

Gentile Inclusion

Separating is always easier than working out a solution. But that was not the vision of the apostles. Theirs was a vision of unity among believers, all together in one accord, in the common fellowship: Brothers and sisters, Jews and Gentiles, worshipping God together, the Israel of God together in the same venue and in the same services. "For he himself is our peace, who has made us both one and has broken down in his flesh the dividing wall of hostility" (Ephesians 2:14). Jewish and Gentile believers are, in the Messiah Yeshua, fellow heirs, joint heirs, sons of the same Father, children of God; and indeed it is true that in Yeshua the Messiah there is neither Jew nor Greek, male nor female, slave nor free.

> So then you are no longer strangers and aliens, but you are fellow citizens with the saints and members of the household of God, built on the foundation of the apostles and prophets, Christ Jesus himself being the cornerstone, in whom the whole structure, being joined together, grows into a holy temple in the Lord. In him you also are being built together into a dwelling place for God by the Spirit. (Ephesians 2:19–22)

The apostolic vision is not one of division. The apostolic vision of worship is not one of one body with many parts and each part of the body having its own prayers and prayer services: the foot prays the foot-prayers and the hand prays the hand-prayers and the eye prays the eye-prayers. When the body of Christ worships the

Father, we are to worship together as one body, with one tongue, with one voice, as one body.

How is this vision of unified prayer to be realized? How is a Gentile supposed to pray Jewish prayers? This is the same question that was being asked nineteen hundred years ago when the Gentile believers first began to participate in the Jewish prayer services. Ultimately, that question, left unanswered, resulted in the exodus of the Gentiles from the synagogue, the jettisoning of Judaism, and the formation of an anti-Jewish mode of worship. And that course of action remains a possibility for us today in the Messianic Jewish movement. We could weed out all the exclusivist language from the *Siddur*. We could take out all those prayers that speak of the Jewish people being chosen and unique. But why stop there? Why not do that to the whole Bible? That language which grants Israel a unique and exalted status is all over the Bible, and you could say it is one of the main ideas of the Bible.

Removing the special elect status of Israel and transferring that status to believers is an unbiblical theological proposition called Replacement Theology. So let's not do that. Let's not edit the people of Israel out of the prayers of Israel.

Messianic Judaism, then, is left with the problem: "How does a Gentile, in good conscience, pray Jewish prayers?" Before I attempt to answer that question, let me tell you a little bit about my own experiences with the problem.

From Phony to Messianic

About fifteen years ago my wife and I began attending a Messianic congregation in Saint Paul. The congregation did a few selections of liturgy: *Mah Tovu*, a part of *Ahavah Rabbah*, a part of the *Shema*, a part of the *Amidah*, the *Oseh Shalom*, and a short Torah service. The congregation expected the men in attendance to wear a prayer shawl (tallit).

I felt phony putting on a tallit on Saturday morning as if I were Jewish, especially when I did not put it on any other day of the week. Neither did I pray morning prayers any other day of the week. In order to legitimize wearing this garment, I bought Hayim Donin's book on Jewish prayer, *To Pray as Jew*, and I read it from cover to cover a few times. Then I purchased a *Siddur* and started praying *shacharit* every morning, donning the tallit every morning. Then I felt that at least I could wear it on Shabbat and not feel like I was just putting it on as a show in the eyes of men. I was wearing the tallit and praying the morning prayers in the privacy of my home six other days of the week, as the Master says:

> "And when you pray, you must not be like the hypocrites. For they love to stand and pray in the synagogues and at the street corners, that they may be seen by others. Truly, I say to you, they have received their reward. But when you pray, go into your room and shut the door and pray to your Father who is in secret. And your Father who sees in secret will reward you." (Matthew 6:5–6)

I never worried much, at first, about the fact that I was not Jewish, because I had not really thought the matter out. I just enjoyed being able to pray along with Israel, and I felt a certain satisfaction knowing that I was praying the same prayers in concert with the nation of Israel. I have been praying these same prayers ever since then, so I have some experience as a Gentile praying Jewish prayers, and I hope to be able to offer some direction for those of you who are not Jewish but have found yourselves in a religion that is.

How does a Gentile, in good conscience, pray Jewish prayers? It is not actually a different question from asking how a Gentile fits into Israel at all. That, in itself, is a difficult question, and there are different answers, opinions, and interpretations even with Messianic Judaism.

To start with, we look to Romans 11 and Paul's metaphor of being grafted into the olive tree. He speaks of wild branches from other olive trees, representing people from other nations, who have been engrafted into the cultivated olive tree—that is, made a part of the greater whole of the nation of Israel. But it is dangerous and unwise to derive halachah (legal rulings) from a metaphor, even if it is in the Scriptures. Even though I am, indeed, grafted into the olive tree of Israel through Messiah, Paul makes it clear that the engrafting is not the same as a legal conversion. Becoming a believer does not make a person legally Jewish. If it did, there would be no questions to be resolved around believers praying Jewish liturgy.

Imagine trying to pray as a Gentile when you come to the blessing that says, "Blessed are you, LORD ... who has not made me a Gentile." That was one of the first things I had to resolve. There is no way around this, but an important rule to remember when praying Jewish liturgy is that the *Siddur* is not the Torah. If a particular prayer makes you feel uncomfortable or if you do not care for a particular blessing, skip it and don't pray it. That is a real and legitimate option. I used to skip the blessing, but one day as I was studying through the book of Acts, writing for *Torah Club Volume Four*, I noticed a relevant passage in Acts 11. After Peter explained to the other apostles his vision of the sheet and his experience with the household of Cornelius the Gentile, he said, "If then God gave the same gift to them as he gave to us when we believed in the Lord Jesus Christ, who was I that I could stand in God's way?" (Acts 11:17). The apostles responded with a blessing and what can be construed to be a liturgical formula:

> When they heard these things they fell silent. And they glorified God, saying, "Then to the Gentiles also God has granted repentance that leads to life." (Acts 11:18)

When Acts 11 says, "They glorified God," it uses the Greek word *doxazo*, a word that sometimes appears in the Apostolic Writings in reference to offering a formula blessing.[192] The *doxazo* that the apostles offered to God follows the form of a typical Jewish blessing by stating something that God did. A typical blessing follows the formula: "Blessed are you LORD, our God, king of the universe, who has done such and such." In this case, the "who has done such and such" would be "who has given to the Gentiles also the repentance to life." So when the question about the who-has-not-made-me-a-Gentile-blessing arose in the process of creating the First Fruits of Zion *Siddur*, it seemed that the apostles had already offered us an alternative right out of the Scriptures:

> Blessed are you LORD, our God, king of the universe, who has granted even to the Gentiles the repentance that leads to life.

Shabbat Kiddush

Acts 11:18 provides a nice alternative for the Gentile praying Jewish liturgy, but that solution does not work in every case. For example, what does the Gentile do when he comes to the Kiddush blessing on Friday night? Imagine the situation. It is Friday night at the Sabbath table, and your family is not Jewish. You are using a *Siddur* to proclaim the holiness of the Sabbath over the *Kiddush* cup when you come to the words that say, "For you chose us and sanctified us from all of the peoples and you caused us to inherit your holy Sabbath with love and favor."

My pedigree is a mix of Irish, English, and Swedish. Those are all fine peoples, but none of them are the chosen people who were sanctified from all of the peoples, and none of them are the inheritors of the holy Sabbath. So this is a problem.

In a situation like this, having the proper *kavanah* is important. The Hebrew word *kavanah* means "intention." When used in regard to prayer, *kavanah* refers to the intention of the heart. For example, when praying liturgy, a person might be reading the words on the page while thinking about a baseball game. That's not good *kavanah*. To pray with *kavanah* requires a person to pray with his mind, to focus on what he is saying, and to intentionally direct his words toward heaven. As the Apostle Paul says, "For if I pray in a tongue, my spirit prays but my mind is unfruitful. What am I to do? I will pray with my spirit, but I will pray with my mind also; I will sing praise with my spirit, but I will sing with my mind also" (1 Corinthians 14:14–15). In Hebrew idiom, the heart is equivalent to the mind. To pray with our hearts means to pray with intention. Prayer is called the service of the heart, which is to say, the worship service of the mind.

A prayer could, in a sense, be regarded as an empty container. The words are empty containers that need to be filled with a person's *kavanah* before they become a prayer. With any liturgical form, it becomes a question of what the person praying intends by the words he or she is praying.

Praying the Friday night *Kiddush* is simply a matter of having the right *kavanah*. Even though I am not ethnically or halachically (legally) a member of the chosen people, nevertheless, through Messiah, I was chosen and sanctified in Messiah. As Paul says,

"God has chosen you from the beginning for salvation through sanctification by the Spirit and faith in the truth" (2 Thessalonians 2:13 NASB). The Gentile brothers and sisters have been chosen from all the peoples. The liturgy of Revelation 5:9 says that the Gentiles believers have been ransomed "from every tribe and language and people and nation" (Revelation 5:9).

Moreover, the traditional Friday night *Kiddush* prayer says, "You caused us to inherit your Holy Sabbath with love and favor." This inheritance theme brings to mind Yeshua's charge to the Apostle Paul. When the Master appeared to Paul in a vision, he told Paul that he was sending him to the Gentiles "that they may receive ... an inheritance among those who have been sanctified by faith in Me" (Acts 26:18 NASB). Along the same lines, Paul speaks of the Gentiles who have, through Messiah, received a "share in the inheritance of the saints in Light" (Colossians 1:12 NASB).

The *Kiddush* prayer speaks of the holy Sabbath as a gift to the people of Israel. This reminds me of the passage in Isaiah (56:6–7) about the Gentiles who take hold of the covenant and keep the Sabbath and are given a name among the people of Israel.

The Gentile believer who prays the Friday night *Kiddush* should keep in mind that he has been chosen from his nation and sanctified in Messiah and given an inheritance with the people of Israel, and that he has voluntarily taken hold of the covenant and the gift of Sabbath. He should keep in mind that, in Messiah, he is privileged to declare the *Kiddush* along with the Jewish people—not in place of the Jewish people, but in concert with them. That *kavanah* allows him to pray the *Kiddush* with full confidence:

> Blessed are you, O LORD, our God, King of the universe, who has sanctified us with his commandments and has shown us favor, and has caused us to inherit his holy Sabbath, with love and favor ... For you chose us and sanctified us from all of the peoples, and you caused us to inherit your holy Sabbath with love and favor.

This is a different intention from what a Jewish person might have in mind while praying the same words. But as a Gentile, so long as I remember to have the proper *kavanah*, I can pray the *Kiddush* without a sense of disingenuousness. Rather, I can be confident of my identity in Yeshua. I am one from the nations, one of those called out from among every people, tribe, and tongue, and one sanctified in Messiah and given an inheritance with the chosen people—even the Holy Sabbath and the covenant it symbolizes. That is my intention when I say the *Kiddush* with my family.

Who Has Sanctified Us with His Commandments

The same concept of *kavanah* applies to the words that begin every blessing over a mitzvah: the oft-repeated formula that says, "who has sanctified us with his commandments." A person might say, "He set apart the Jews with his commandments because he gave the Torah to Israel, but he did not set apart the Gentiles with the commandments, therefore it is not appropriate for a Gentile believer to pray the words, 'Who has sanctified us with his commandments.'" Again, this is a matter of proper *kavanah*. When I pray a blessing like that, I do not mean that God has set apart the Irish, English, or Swedish with his commandments. Instead, I am including myself in the people of Israel. My intention is to pray along with that greater collective of Israel as a fellow heir. I am a Gentile who has also been set apart along with the nation of Israel because I have been grafted into this people. My intention is not to claim Jewish status, but to acknowledge my place with the greater people of Israel in Messiah.

God of Our Fathers

A person might ask, "How can a Gentile pray the words 'God of my fathers, God of Abraham, Isaac, and Jacob?'" This question is answered in the writings of the Apostle Paul. In the book of Galatians, Paul tells the Gentile believers, "If you are Christ's, then you are Abraham's offspring, heirs according to promise" (Galatians 3:29). When Paul calls us sons of Abraham (*benei Avraham*), that is not to the exclusion of the other fathers, Isaac and Jacob. To be a son of Abraham (*ben Avraham*) is terminology in the Jewish community for being a proselyte, adopted into the people.

A proselyte to Judaism named Obadiah once struggled with the same questions of paternity. He was vexed by the opening words of the *Amidah* prayer, which says, "Blessed are you, O LORD, our God and God of our fathers, the God of Abraham, the God of Isaac, and the God of Jacob." Obadiah felt that he was not entitled to pray those words because he was not a natural-born Jew. He wrote to the famous rabbi Maimonides for advice.

Maimonides's response (quoted earlier in this book) was as follows:

> Anyone who becomes a convert throughout the generations and anyone who unifies the Name of the Holy One as it is written in the Torah is a disciple of our father Abraham, and all of them are members of his household … Hence you may say: "Our God and God of our fathers," for Abraham, peace be upon him, is your father … Because you have come beneath the wings of the Divine Presence and attached yourself to God, there is no difference between us and you … You certainly may recite the blessings, 'Who has chosen us,' 'Who has given us,' 'Who has caused us to inherit' and 'Who has separated us,' for the Creator has already chosen you and has separated you from the nations and has given you the Torah.[193]

Maimonides was not speaking about Gentile believers. He was speaking about someone who had made a full, legal conversion to Judaism. Nevertheless, the same principle should apply to any believer who has taken shelter beneath the wings of the Divine Presence. This was certainly the apostolic opinion of Gentile believers. For example, in 1 Corinthians 10, while speaking to Gentile believers, Paul refers even to the generation in the wilderness as "our fathers." If the generation that perished in the wilderness could be called the fathers of the Gentile believers, how much more should Abraham, Isaac, and Jacob? In the epistle of Clement, the disciple Clement, who was himself a Gentile believer so far as we know, referred not only to both Abraham as "our father" but also to Jacob.[194]

When we are grafted into Israel, we are adopted into Israel, and when adopted, we share the same grandparents. If prayed with the correct kavanah—the intention that we are children of Abraham, Isaac, and Jacob because we are in Messiah, and he is the seed of Abraham, and we have been engrafted into the commonwealth of Israel, and we understand that Abraham, Isaac, and Jacob are the fathers of our faith—it is completely appropriate for a Gentile believer to say, "God of our fathers, God of Abraham, God of Isaac."

GATHER OUR EXILES

A little further on in the weekday *Amidah* prayer, the Gentile might stumble over the petition pertaining to the ingathering of Israel:

> Blast the great shofar for our freedom and lift a banner to gather our exiles, and gather us together from the four corners of the earth. Blessed are you O LORD, who gathers the scattered ones of Israel.

This blessing refers to the eschatological ingathering of Israel promised by the prophets. Judaism anticipates that when Messiah comes, he will sound a great trumpet and gather the Jewish people back to land of Israel. Even the ten lost tribes will be included in this end-times ingathering. The Gentile believer encountering this part of the prayers might think, "How can I refer to the exile of Israel in the first person as if I am one of the scattered people of Israel? I am not living in exile."

That may be true, but Paul nonetheless included Gentile believers in the messianic ingathering:

> For the Lord himself will descend from heaven with a cry of command, with the voice of an archangel, and with the sound of the trumpet of God. And the dead in Christ will rise first. Then we who are alive, who are left, will be caught up together with them in the clouds to meet the Lord in the air, and so we will always be with the Lord. Therefore encourage one another with these words. (1 Thessalonians 4:16–18)

Paul included the Gentile believers of Thessalonica in the midst of the great end-times ingathering of Israel. From Paul's perspective, it is completely appropriate for the Gentile believer to pray for the "ingathering of our exiles" in the first person. Similarly, in the late first-century document called the *Didache*, apostolic-era writers prescribe very similar prayers for Gentile believers:

> May your assembly be gathered from the ends of the earth into your kingdom.

Gather the betrothed from the four winds to your kingdom that you have prepared for her. (*Didache* 9:4, 10:5)

THE UNCIRCUMCISED SHALL NOT ABIDE

One of the most problematic pieces of liturgy that a Gentile believer might encounter in the traditional Jewish liturgy is the blessing in the Sabbath morning *Amidah* that explicitly excludes Gentiles from participation in the Sabbath. Immediately after reciting the declaration in Exodus 31:16–17 that the Sabbath is an eternal sign between God and Israel, the *Amidah* reads as follows:

> And you did not give it, O LORD, our God, to the nations of the lands, and you did not cause the servants of idols to inherit it, and in its rest the uncircumcised shall not abide, for you gave it to Israel with love, to the seed of Jacob whom you chose.

Nothing is wrong with this blessing. It is absolutely true. God did give the Sabbath to Israel and not to the other nations. If a Gentile believer opts to keep the Sabbath as an expression of his faith in Messiah, he must remember that the Sabbath was not given to him; it was given to Israel. His participation in the Sabbath is only possible through his association with the Messiah of Israel.

However, it might feel uncomfortable for an uncircumcised Gentile to pray the words, "And in its rest the uncircumcised shall not abide." But remember that in the writings of the Apostle Paul, uncircumcised Gentile believers are included within the greater commonwealth of Israel. They are not legal Israel or, in his language, Israel-according-to-the-flesh, but Paul includes uncircumcised Gentile believers in what he calls the commonwealth of Israel, the Israel of God, the one new man. In that regard, he grants the Gentiles an honorary status with Israel. Paul says, "For neither circumcision counts for anything nor uncircumcision, but keeping the commandments of God" (1 Corinthians 7:19). The uncircumcised Gentile who rests in Messiah, in Paul's words, has undergone a circumcision of the heart:

> In him also you were circumcised with a circumcision made without hands, by putting off the body of the flesh, by the circumcision of Christ, having been buried with

him in baptism, in which you were also raised with him through faith in the powerful working of God, who raised him from the dead. (Colossians 2:11–12)

Again, proper *kavanah* is the key to praying Jewish liturgy. An uncircumcised Gentile who prays the words "In its rest the uncircumcised shall not abide" need only remember that he is circumcised in heart and rests in Messiah.

So then, there remains a Sabbath rest for the people of God, for whoever has entered God's rest has also rested from his works as God did from his. (Hebrews 4:9–10)

Church and Synagogue

The controversial blessings and potential solutions for Gentile believers that I have offered above are only a sampling. Several more examples could be offered. But why should a Gentile be concerned with praying Jewish liturgy in the first place?

In the apostolic communities, fellowship between the Gentile and Jewish believers was a major concern. The apostles seemed to have no intention of creating a bilateral ecclesiology whereby God would have two different peoples: his Gentile people, the church; and his Jewish people, Israel.

Nevertheless, that concept has gained momentum in Messianic Judaism today. Many feel that Jews should do the Jewish stuff—pray the Jewish prayers and keep the Torah—while Gentiles should do Christian stuff and go to church and, for the most part, stay out of the Messianic synagogue. Jews and Gentiles should mutually edify each other, recognizing that they are different parts of the same body: Israel and the church.

But that's not one body with many parts. That's two bodies. That is not one people; it is two peoples. That is not one new man; it is two men. It is not a spiritual house being built on the foundation of Christ and the apostles; it is two different houses.

Do not misunderstand: I am not against the church existing as a separate entity with its own integrity, rituals, and institutions. But I am saying that the Messianic synagogue has to learn to accommodate Gentile believers who desire to live and practice their faith in a manner consistent with Torah and Judaism. Messianic Judaism cannot close its doors to the Gentiles. To do so would be to repeat the mistakes of the past. The apostolic-era, Messianic synagogue was a place where Jew and Gentile worshipped together, praying the same prayers, hearing the same Scriptures, studying the same Torah, enjoying the same fellowship, and breaking the same bread. They lived together in the common bond of the Holy Spirit. They were one body with many parts—Jew and Gentile, fellow heirs—praying together.

But when it comes to the question of which religion (Is ours a Jewish or Gentile religion?) and which prayers (Are they Jewish or Gentile prayers?), we have to agree with Paul, who says that the Scriptures, the worship, and the services were all given into the charge and safekeeping of the Jewish people:

> They are Israelites, and to them belong the adoption, the glory, the covenants, the giving of the law, the worship, and the promises. To them belong the patriarchs, and from their race, according to the flesh, is the Christ who is God over all, blessed forever. Amen. (Romans 9:4–5)

SUMMARY

To pray as a Gentile, in some cases, might mean skipping blessings with which we are uncomfortable or that do not apply to us. It might sometimes mean adding blessings derived directly from the Scriptures, such as "who has given even to the Gentiles the repentance unto life." More often, though, praying Jewish liturgy as a Gentile is a matter of praying with correct *kavanah.* For example, it is completely appropriate for a Gentile to pray the words "For you chose us and sanctified us from all of the peoples and you caused us to inherit your holy Sabbath with love and favor," so long as the Gentile is thinking, "Indeed, I have been chosen in Messiah, sanctified in Messiah, taken as an individual from among all the peoples and given this gracious gift of an inheritance with the people of my beloved Savior, Yeshua."

Sometimes Gentiles in the Messianic synagogue feel a second-class status. They feel that if only they could become Jewish, it would validate their participation there. As for me, I am proud to be one gathered from the nations and joined to the people through Messiah.

I do agree with the Chabad rabbi who told my friend that the prayers of the synagogue and *Siddur* are not appropriate for Gentiles. But a believing Gentile is not just a Gentile. A believing Gentile is an adjunct member of Israel, grafted into the olive tree, a son of Abraham by faith. A believing Gentile is not just a Gentile. In the words of the Apostle Peter, the believing Gentiles have become a "chosen race, a royal priesthood, a holy nation, a people for his own possession."

> But you are a chosen race, a royal priesthood, a holy nation, a people for his own possession, that you may proclaim the excellencies of him who called you out of darkness into his marvelous light. Once you were not a people, but now you are God's people; once you had not received mercy, but now you have received mercy. (1 Peter 2:9–10)

BIBLIOGRAPHY

Attridge, Harold W., and Gohei Hata, eds. *Eusebius, Christianity, and Judaism*. Detroit, MI: Wayne State University Press, 1992.

Bagatti, Bellarmino. *The Church from the Circumcision*. Jerusalem: Franciscan Printing Press, 1984.

Berkowitz, Ariel and D'vorah, *Take Hold*. Littleton, CO: First Fruits of Zion, 1999.

Berkowitz, Ariel and D'vorah. *Torah Rediscovered*. Littleton, CO: First Fruits of Zion, 1996.

Bruce, F. F. *The Book of Acts*. Grand Rapids, MI: Eerdmans, 1988.

Charlesworth, James H. *The Old Testament Pseudepigrapha*. 2 vols. New York: Doubleday, 1983.

Chasidah, Yishai. *Encyclopedia of Biblical Personalities*. Jerusalem: Shaar Press, 1994.

Daube, David. *The New Testament and Rabbinic Judaism*. Great Britain: University of London, The Athlone Press, 1956.

Flusser, David. *Judaism and the Origins of Christianity*. Jerusalem: The Magnes Press, 1998.

Gaston, Lloyd. *Paul and the Torah*. Vancouver, Canada: University of British Columbia Press, 1987.

Hegg, Tim. *It is Often Said: Comments and Comparisons of Evangelical Thought & Hebraic Theology*. Marshfield, MO: First Fruits of Zion, 2003.

Hegg, Tim. *The Letter Writer: Paul's Background and Torah Perspective*. Marshfield, MO: First Fruits of Zion, 2002.

Kaplan, Aryeh. *Waters of Eden: The Mystery of the Mikvah*. Brooklyn, NY: Mesorah Publications, 2000.

Kling, Simcha. *Embracing Judaism*. New York: The Rabbinical Assembly, 1976.

Lachs, Samuel Tobias. *A Rabbinic Commentary on the New Testament*. Hoboken, NJ: Ktav Publishing House, 1987.

Metford, J. C. J. *Dictionary of Christian Lore and Legend*. London: Thames and Hudson, 1983.

Patai, Raphael. *The Messiah Texts*. Detroit, MI: Wayne State University Press, 1988.

Pixner, Bargil. "Church of the Apostles Found on Mount Zion." *Biblical Archaeological Review* 16:2 (May/June 1990): 17–35, 60.

Pritz, Ray. *Nazarene Jewish Christianity*. Jerusalem: The Magnes Press, 1992.

Scherman, Nosson, *The Stone Edition Chumash*. Brooklyn, NY: Mesorah Publications Ltd., 1994.

Scherman, Nosson and Meir Zlotowitz, *Bereishis: A New Translation with a Commentary Anthologized from Talmudic, Midrashic, and Rabbinic Sources*. Brooklyn, NY: Mesorah Publications Ltd., 1986.

Whiston, William. *The New Complete Works of Josephus*. Grand Rapids, MI: Kregel Publications, 1999.

Williamson, G. A. *Eusebius: The History of the Church*. Minneapolis, MN: Augsburg Publishing, 1965.

Young, Brad. *Jesus the Jewish Theologian*. Peabody, MA: Hendrickson Publishers, 1995.

Young, Brad. *The Parables: Jewish Tradition and Christian Interpretation*. Peabody, MA: Hendrickson Publishers, 1998.

Zetterholm, Magnus. *The Formation of Christianity in Antioch: A Social-Scientific Approach to the Separation between Judaism and Christianity*. London: Routledge Tayor & Francis Group, 2005.

ENDNOTES

Introduction to the Second Edition

1   Acts 2:11.

Introduction to the First Edition (Revised)

2   m.*Bikkurim* 3:2. The Mishnah is the written code of early Jewish legal traditions, sometimes referred to as the "Oral Law."

3   Philo, *On Laws* 1:96.

4   Ephesians 6:19–20.

Chapter 1

5   Acts 21:20.

6   Acts 21:28.

7   Acts 21:29.

8   *Jewish War* 5:5:2.

9   *Antiquities* 15:11:5.

10   Gamaliel, Paul's tutor in Torah, is a well-known character from Jewish literature. He was a sage known for his wisdom and piety. In Paul's day, he was the president of the Sanhedrin.

11   Tim Hegg notes that Paul's concept of the Gentile inclusion equaling the gospel must be what is meant by his peculiar use of the phrase "my gospel" (Romans 2:16, 16:25; 2 Timothy 2:8); i.e., the inclusion of the Gentiles as revealed to Paul (as described in Ephesians 3). This also helps explain the term "enemies of the gospel" in Romans 11:28. It is not that the people of Israel are enemies of the essence of the gospel (i.e., the means of salvation through God's Messiah). Their aversion to the gospel was a reaction against the inclusion of the Gentiles, which, to Paul, is part and parcel of the gospel message. Thus, they are not called "enemies of the gospel" but "enemies of the gospel *on your account.*" It is not the gospel *per se* that they are against, but the inclusion of the Gentiles.

12   Acts 13:42–43.

13   Acts 13:26.

14   Acts 13:26.

15   Acts 13:44.

16   Acts 13:45.

17   Acts 17:4–5.

18   Ephesians 6:19–20.

19   Acts 22:21.

CHAPTER 2

20   *Genesis Rabbah* 39:11.

21   Romans 4:16–17.

22   Galatians 6:15.

23   *Genesis Rabbah* 39:11.

24   Romans 6:3.

25   Ephesians 2:12–13, italics added.

26   *Torah Temimah* (Nosson Scherman and Meir Zlotowitz, *Bereishis: A New Translation with a Commentary Anthologized from Talmudic, Midrashic, and Rabbinic Sources* [2 vols.; Brooklyn, NY: Mesorah Publications, 1988], 1:435).

27   This opinion is based on a grammatical anomaly in Genesis 12:3. Nowhere else in the Torah does the verb "bless" (*barach*) appear in the form (*niphal*) that it appears in Genesis 12:3. The same verbal root, however, is commonly found in this form in regard to "grafting" of plants (Scherman and Zlotowitz, *Bereishis*, 432).

28   Deuteronomy 23:3.

29   Genesis 15:6.

30   Genesis 22:17–18.

31   The Hebrew *zerah* (seed) is a collective singular. (Its one plural form, 1 Samuel 8:15, is an anomaly.)

32   Galatians 3:26–29.

33   Romans 11:28–29.

CHAPTER 3

34   *Midrash Aggadah, Bereishit* 41:45; *Yalkut Shimoni, Vayishlach* 134 (Yishai Chasidah, *Encyclopedia of Biblical Personalities* [Jerusalem: Shaar Press, 1994], 97–98).

35   *Pirkei d'Rabbi Eliezer* 36.

36   *Joseph and Asenath* 6:5 (Charlesworth).

37   *Joseph and Asenath* 14:9 (Charlesworth).

38   *Joseph and Asenath* 15:2–7 (Charlesworth).

39   *Joseph and Asenath* 21:4 (Charlesworth).

40 However, Burchard's introduction to the work claims that "every competent scholar has confirmed that *Joseph and Asenath* is Jewish" (Charlesworth, *The Old Testament Pseudepigrapha,* 2:186). The majority of scholars maintain that *Joseph and Asenath* is a Jewish work, too Jewish to be written by a Christian. But the rigid distinction we assume between Judaism and Christianity did not exist through most of the first century. It is possible that the author of *Joseph and Asenath* was a Jewish believer.

41 *Joseph and Asenath* 8:9 (Charlesworth).

CHAPTER 4

42 The relationship between Joseph and Yeshua is highlighted from extra-biblical Jewish traditions. The *Midrash Rabbah* tells us that Joseph did not drink of the fruit of the vine from the time he was separated from his brothers until he was reunited with them (*Genesis Rabbah* 93:7). It also informs us that they cast lots for Joseph's coat (*Genesis Rabbah* 84:8). The Testament of Zebulun tells us that Joseph was in the cistern for three days and three nights (*Testament of Zebulun* 4:4). For a more thorough exposition of the parallels between the Joseph narrative and Messiah, see *Torah Club Volume Two: Shadows of the Messiah* (Marshfield, MO: First Fruits of Zion, 2005).

43 Chofetz Chaim (Nosson Scherman, *The Stone Edition Chumash* [Brooklyn, NY: Mesorah Publications, 1994], 253).

44 Genesis 45:4–5.

45 Romans 11:12.

46 Genesis 45:6–8.

47 b.*Sukkot* 52a.

CHAPTER 5

48 Genesis 48:3–4, translating *kehilat amim* as "community of nations."

49 Genesis 48:5.

50 Genesis 48:7–8.

51 Genesis 48:9.

52 Genesis 48:8–11.

53 Genesis 48:15–16.

54 Genesis 48:19.

55 Genesis 48:20.

56 Genesis 48:8.

57 Ephesians 2:19.

58 Ephesians 1:5.

59 Galatians 4:5.

60 Ephesians 3:6.

61 Romans 11:17.

62 Hebrews 2:11–17.

63 Romans 9:4.

64 Genesis 48:19.

65 Galatians 3:29.

66 A textual comparison of Romans 11:25 and Genesis 48:19 raises the possibility that Paul was directly alluding to this passage of Torah. However, if he was, he did not use the LXX wording of the passage, which translates it as "a multitude of nations." Paul's wording is a more literal rendering of the Hebrew.

67 It is not meant to be taken in a literal sense, because the promise of all nations being blessed in "the seed" is already literally fulfilled in Messiah. The Ephraim allusion of Romans 11:25 is not a reference to the physical descendents of Abraham or Ephraim, but rather to those who belong to Messiah.

68 1 Corinthians 11:24, emphasis mine.

69 Exodus 12:48 does specify that "no uncircumcised male" may make a Passover sacrifice or eat of a Passover sacrifice. This prohibition applies equally to uncircumcised Jews and Gentiles. It does not, however, mean that an uncircumcised person cannot celebrate Passover or participate in the Seder or the Feast of Unleavened Bread. It is a prohibition specific only to sacrificing a Passover lamb and eating thereof; thus it is a non-factor outside of a Temple context.

70 1 Corinthians 5:7–8.

71 Genesis 15:13–14.

72 Genesis 50:24.

73 Exodus 6:6–7.

74 Exodus 5:2.

75 Exodus 12:38.

76 Exodus 14:10.

77 Exodus 14:11.

78 Aryeh Kaplan, *Waters of Eden: The Mystery of the Mikvah* (Brooklyn, New York: Mesorah Publications, Ltd., 2000), 11–14.

79 Nakdimon ben Gurion of rabbinic lore. See for example b.*Ta'anit* 19b–20a, b.*Ketubot* 65a-67a, b.*Gittin* 56a, and b.*Avodah Zarah* 25a.

80 b.*Yevamot* 47b.

81 Exodus 15:11.

82 1 Corinthians 5:7, 11:23–31.

83 Psalm 77:20.

84 Psalm 80:1.

85 Certainly the gospel manuscripts are older than the written midrash, but the oral tradition behind a story like this might be ancient. We

can only be certain one version is dependent on the other. For a parallel to Yeshua's parable see Ezekiel 34.

86 Matthew 15:24.

87 Luke 5:31.

88 Luke 15:1–2.

89 Luke 15:4–7.

90 Matthew 10:5–6. This is contrary to a popular interpretation in Two-House theology. By virtue of elimination, Matthew 10:5–6 disqualifies Gentiles (and even those who might only appear to be Gentiles) and Samaritans from being regarded as "lost sheep of Israel" in the gospel sense. If it actually was the lost tribes of Israel that the Master meant for his disciples to go to, he should have sent his disciples to the Gentiles and the Samaritans. The Samaritans, even by the biblical record, are interbred with the lost tribes. Instead He sends them only to Jewish people who know that they are Jews.

91 Matthew 15:24.

92 Luke 7:4–5.

93 Luke 7:6.

94 See John 18:28, Acts 10:28, and m.*Oholot* 18:7.

95 Luke 7:7.

96 Luke 7:9.

97 Matthew 8:11–12.

98 Romans 11:23.

99 Matthew 28:19–20.

100 Ibid.

101 Ibid.

102 Implicitly throughout his ministry, explicitly in Matthew 5:17–20.

CHAPTER 8

103 Exodus 6:7.

104 *Pirke de Rabbi Eliezer* 41. See also *Exodus Rabbah* 43:7, *Numbers Rabbah* 21:2, *Deuteronomy Rabbah* 1:2, 3:12. Compare John 3:29–30.

105 Exodus 19:8.

106 Ephesians 2:12.

107 Exodus 19:5–6.

108 Psalm 68:11.

109 Deuteronomy 27:8.

110 m.*Sotah* 7:5.

111 Romans 3:29.

112 Jeremiah 23:29.

113 *Midrash Chazit* (Moshe Weissman, *The Midrash Says: Shemos*

[Brooklyn, NY: Benei Yakov Publications, 1995], 182).

[114] Psalm 68:11.

[115] Acts 2:5.

[116] Acts 11:1–2.

[117] Acts 10:34–35.

[118] For a thorough explanation of the vision of the sheet, see *Torah Club Volume Four* (Marshfield, MO: First Fruits of Zion, 2002), comments on Acts 10.

[119] Acts 10:36.

[120] Acts 10:28.

[121] Acts 10:45–46.

[122] Acts 10:47.

[123] b.*Yevamot* 47b–48b.

[124] 1 Peter 1:14.

[125] 1 Peter 4:3.

[126] 1 Peter 1:1.

[127] 1 Peter 1:23.

[128] 1 Peter 2:2.

[129] 1 Peter 1:23.

[130] 1 Peter 2:12.

[131] 1 Peter 2:9.

[132] Hosea 1:10.

[133] 1 Peter 2:10. Though Peter used these prophetic passages about the ten northern tribes metaphorically to speak of the Gentile inclusion, the Gentiles he was writing to were real Gentiles and not lost Israelites. Contrary to some Two-House teachings, Peter's readers were "former Gentiles," not "former Israelites." They were born of "imperishable seed" planted through "the word of God," not of natural seed born of Israelite descent. Their forefathers were not described as the noble patriarchs Abraham, Isaac, and Jacob, but as pagans who handed on an "empty way of life." His readers were "reborn," not "returned." They were Gentiles from among the nations of the world.

CHAPTER 9

[134] Acts 15:5.

[135] Acts 15:7.

[136] Acts 15:8–11.

[137] Acts 15:13–19.

[138] Acts 15:20–21.

[139] Acts 15:21.

140 The formulation of the nineteenth benediction (a curse against
   believers) by the council at Yavneh around 95 CE implies that
   believers were still in the synagogues even at the close of the first
   century.

141 Acts 15:17.

142 According to b.*Sanhedrin* 96b–97a, David's restored tent is identified
   as Messiah.

CHAPTER 10

143 Galatians 1:8–9.

144 Galatians 5:12.

145 1 Corinthians 7:19.

146 Galatians 3:3.

147 Galatians 5:2.

148 1 Corinthians 7:18.

149 Acts 21:21.

150 Romans 4:16.

151 *Maimonides's Letter to Obadiah the Proselyte* (Simcha Kling,
   Embracing Judaism [New York: The Rabbinical Assembly, 1987], 4).

152 Galatians 3:28.

153 1 Corinthians 6:15.

154 John 14:20.

155 2 Corinthians 5:17.

156 Galatians 6:15–16.

CHAPTER 11

157 Psalm 122:1–2.

158 Josephus, *Jewish War* 5:5:2.

159 Josephus, *Antiquities* 15:11:5.

160 Ephesians 2:12.

161 Ephesians 2:13.

162 Ephesians 2:9.

163 Ephesians 2:8.

164 For example, compare the King James Version on the passage.

165 Ephesians 2:15–17.

166 Ephesians 2:19.

167 Ezekiel 37.

168 Ephesians 2:21–22.

169 Ephesians 3:1.

170 Ephesians 3:3.

171 Ephesians 3:11.

172 Ephesians 3:10.

173 Isaiah 49:6.

174 Revelation 7:9.

EPILOGUE

175 Isaiah 11:10.

176 Isaiah 51:4–5.

177 Isaiah 56: 7.

178 Isaiah 49:22–25.

179 Exodus 31:17.

180 Isaiah 60:3–4.

181 Isaiah 62:10.

ADDITIONAL CHAPTER 1

182 Bellarmino Bagatti, *The Church from the Circumcision* (Jerusalem: Franciscan Printing Press, 1984), 125.

183 Eusebius, *Ecclesiastical History* 1.7.13–14.

184 Bagatti, *The Church from the Circumcision*, 116–122; Bargil Pixner, "Church of the Apostles Found on Mount Zion," *Biblical Archaeological Review* 16:2 (May/June 1990): 17–35, 60.

185 Ibid.

186 Ibid.

187 Magnus Zetterholm, *The Formation of Christianity in Antioch: A Social-Scientific Approach to the Separation between Judaism and Christianity* (London: Routledge Tayor & Francis Group, 2005), 37–38.

188 Zetterholm, *The Formation of Christianity in Antioch*, 91–95.

189 Ray Pritz, *Nazarene Jewish Christianity* (Jerusalem: The Magnes Press, 1992), 48–70.

190 Epiphanius, *Panarion* 29:7, 5.

ADDITIONAL CHAPTER 2

191 Galatians 3:28. Interpreting Galatians 3:28 as a halachic standard is untenable because that would mean the inverse was also true, that all Jews must be Greeks—not to mention that distinctions between men and women, slave and free would also need be obliterated.

192 David Flusser, *Judaism and the Origins of Christianity* (Jerusalem: The Magnes Press, 1998), 535–542.

193 *Maimonides's Letter to Obadiah the Proselyte* (Kling, *Embracing Judaism*, 4). See also chapter 10 of this book.

194 1 Clement 4:8, 31:2.